CASE STUDIES IN CULTURAL

ANTHROPOLOGY

SERIES EDITORS

George and Louise Spindler

STANFORD UNIVERSITY

---

# THE LUGBARA OF UGANDA

Second Edition

# The Lugbara Of Uganda

Second Edition

John Middleton

CENGAGE
Learning·

Australia · Brazil · Japan · Korea · Mexico · Singapore · Spain · United Kingdom · United States

**The Lugbara Of Uganda: Second Edition**

John Middleton

Executive Editor:
Michele Baird
Maureen Staudt
Michael Stranz

Project Development Editor:
Linda de Stefano

Senior Marketing Coordinators:
Sara Mercurio

Lindsay Shapiro

Production/Manufacturing Manager:
Donna M. Brown

PreMedia Services Supervisor:
Rebecca A. Walker

Rights & Permissions Specialist:
Kalina Hintz

Cover Image:
Getty Images*

© 2008, 2002 Cengage Learning

For product information and technology assistance, contact us at
**Cengage Learning Customer & Sales Support, 1-800-354-9706**

For permission to use material from this text or product,
submit all requests online at **cengage.com/permissions**
Further permissions questions can be emailed to
**permissionrequest@cengage.com**

ISBN-13: 978-0-534-96895-3

ISBN-10: 0-534-96895-3

**Cengage Learning**
5191 Natorp Boulevard
Mason, Ohio 45040
USA

Cengage Learning is a leading provider of customized learning solutions with office locations around the globe, including Singapore, the United Kingdom, Australia, Mexico, Brazil, and Japan. Locate your local office at:
**international.cengage.com/region**

Cengage Learning products are represented in Canada by Nelson Education, Ltd.

For your lifelong learning solutions, visit **custom.cengage.com**

Visit our corporate website at **cengage.com**

Printed in the United States of America

# Foreword

## ABOUT THE SERIES

These case studies in cultural anthropology are designed for students in beginning and intermediate courses in the social sciences, to bring them insights into the richness and complexity of human life as it is lived in different ways, in different places. The authors are men and women who have lived in the societies they write about and who are professionally trained as observers and interpreters of human behavior. Also, the authors are teachers; in their writing, the needs of the student reader remain foremost. It is our belief that when an understanding of ways of life very different from one's own is gained, abstractions and generalizations about the human condition become meaningful.

The scope and character of the series has changed constantly since we published the first case studies in 1960, in keeping with our intention to represent anthropology as it is. We are concerned with the ways in which human groups and communities are coping with the massive changes wrought in their physical and sociopolitical environments in recent decades. We are also concerned with the ways in which established cultures have solved life's problems. And we want to include representation of the various modes of communication and emphasis that are being formed and reformed as anthropology itself changes.

We think of this series as an instructional series, intended for use in the classroom. We, the editors, have always used case studies in our teaching, whether for beginning students or advanced graduate students. We start with case studies, whether from our own series or from elsewhere, and weave our way into theory, and then turn again to cases. For us, they are the grounding of our discipline.

## ABOUT THE AUTHOR

John Middleton received his doctorate from the University of Oxford, where his teachers included E. E. Evans-Pritchard, Max Gluckman, and Meyer Fortes. He has carried out field research among the Lugbara, the Swahili of Zanzibar and Kenya, the Igbo in Lagos, and the Eastern Akan of Akuapem, Ghana. He has published *The Kikuyu and Kamba of Kenya* (1953), *Lugbara Religion* (1960), *Land Tenure in Zanzibar* (1961), *The Effects of Economic Development on Political Systems in Africa* (1966), *The Study of the Lugbara* (1970), *The World of the Swahili* (in press); this book is a revision of *The Lugbara of Uganda* (1965); he has also edited several books and published many papers, mostly on the Lugbara. He has taught at London,

Cape Town, Northwestern, and New York Universities and since 1981 has been Professor of Anthropology and Religious Studies at Yale University.

Acknowledgements for help with the original edition of this book were given in the 1965 edition. For help in this revision he wishes to thank Michelle Gilbert, Elizabeth Cakuru, and Timothy Allen.

## ABOUT THIS CASE STUDY

The author gives the reader a clear picture of the setting of Lugbara behavior in the first chapter, and then leads directly to an analysis of how the Lugbara conceive of their society. In this analysis the spatial dimensions of their social relationships, the lay of their land and the distribution of their dwellings, and their social system are linked with the myths that gave these sociospatial relationships depth in time and special meaning. In this way, one gains a functional view of Lugbara society, and one sees how every aspect of Lugbara life—fighting, marriage, the settling of disputes, the disposal of the dead and mourning for them, the exercise of leadership and authority—was interdependent with every other aspect.

It is particularly noteworthy that until very recently the Lugbara settled most important disputes by feud or warfare, but that despite a traditional form of social organization that was highly fragmented and lacked obvious political authority above the local group level, and a high density of population, they were able to control competition between local groups for land, grazing, and water. In this respect, and in others, the Lugbara present an interesting contrast to the Banyoro, described by John Beattie, and the Swazi, described by Hilda Kuper, for these two societies are held together by a strongly centralized state organization.

After Ugandan independence in 1962 the fate of the Lugbara took a turn for the worse, briefly described in the last chapter of this revision. For a time, they enjoyed greater representation in positions of authority only to have the situation reversed in a few years. A time of severe harassment and wholesale murder followed. Then, as refugees their lot was desperate, since they sought refuge during a time of starvation—famine was sweeping the land, and under these conditions there was no haven for them anywhere. The society and culture as described by John Middleton are no more. We are fortunate to have this record of a significant way of life available to students.

George and Louise Spindler
Series Editors
Ethnographics
P.O. Box 38
Calistoga CA 94515

# Preface to Revised Edition

The original version of this book was written in the early 1960s, and was intended to be a brief descriptive account of the Lugbara during the time I lived among them between December 1949 and September 1953. In it I used the "ethnographic present" tense, for the simple reason that at that time Lugbara society did not appear to be structurally very different from what the people themselves considered "traditional"; this was their view and I followed it. It was, of course, an anthropological commonplace of the time that the notion of "traditional" has many flaws if used to refer to a believed-unchanging culture. Today many anthropologists, historians, and others happily beat away at the long-dead horse of the notion of "traditional cultures," but the term's usage, then conventional in ethnographic narrative, was not at the time so misleading as fashionable and historically insensitive critics of ethnography believe. All societies change continually, but they may do so only very slowly. All African societies have altered to a remarkable extent in the last twenty or thirty years, but changes before then were generally far more gradual. Ethnographers have only rarely assumed small-scale societies on the fringes of the capitalist world to be without historical change, and have always taken note of the social and historical contexts provided by their exploited and subordinate position in world economy. They have not been unaware of history but have been unsure of how to use it, a very different matter.

The notion of the "traditional" has value, both for the people themselves and for the anthropologist. It refers essentially to a society whose underlying social structure has been relatively unchanging for a long period, whose members accept that their children will lead basically the same lives as themselves, where the knowledge of experience by different ages and ranks is relatively unchanging and foreseeable, and where the past is always in the present. These closely related characteristics are of course relative, often difficult to define or to measure, yet they have valid significance and utility.

I need not discuss social structure here except to say that it is a system of relations of power and authority as conceived by a group of people who define their group as an entity that exercises that power, and who accept that orderly succession to authority over time is assured by custom. Succession to rights of authority over time and generation is important. In a "traditional" society this succession is accepted as ordained and foreseeable. The fact that this is seldom observably true is irrelevant; we are discussing peoples' views of structure and tradition. This assuredness that the future will be similar to the past, and the certainty of one's children's roles, may of course be affected by differences of rank, wealth, political authority, religion, gender, and literacy. With this assuredness goes the knowledge appropriate to a given status—knowledge that is passed on as immaculately as possible to following generations. A society may change from one view of "traditional" to another at times of radical, structural, and qualitative change.

The point is that the "traditional" for the Lugbara people of the 1950s was vitally important to them and in general was accepted to have changed little since the limits of human pre-literate recall, before the period of colonial rule. Changes since that time—and many were recognized—were seen as essentially minor and temporary upsets that could still be dealt with by "traditional" means (even if I, as an observer, realized they could not be). The then-very few Christian and educated Lugbara thought differently. But in contrast to, say, the Kikuyu of Kenya, who had long realized that their "traditional" society had been destroyed by colonial rule and that the only recourse was to build a new one altogether—if necessary by force and revolution—the Lugbara looked to their past as something they could still retain and cherish. Today this view may no longer be held by those who have survived the terrors and cruelties of Amin and Obote, but it is hard to believe that they hold no views, perhaps expressed in a mythopoeic ideology, of the "perfection" of their society's past.

It is in this sense that I wrote about the "traditional," and it was in this sense that I used the "ethnographic present" tense, except for a few situations where change was clearly apparent (as in the cessation of feud and warfare). Since that time, however, much of what I saw and tried to describe and understand of everyday behavior has vanished forever, and so I have changed the tense used throughout this book.

In the original book I used phrases such as "The Lugbara do such-and-such" or "The Lugbara say so-and-so." This was of course a simplification. There seems no point in attributing *verbatim* remarks to particular people when those remarks are made by all, or virtually all, people, or when they take standard forms of expression that I would hear almost daily. It must be remembered that at that time, at least, people of the same sex and age followed remarkably similar routines and expressed very similar thoughts and ideas on the public occasions to which I referred. Norms of social behavior were strong.

However, this said, I did ignore the cultural variations in different parts of the country, a feature I addressed in a later publication (Middleton 1968b). Lugbara themselves made little of these variations, which they saw as interesting diacritical differences between clans and parts of the country. They correctly saw the underlying structure as being the same everywhere, so my usage does not distort the main trend of this brief descriptive account.

Some critics objected that the book included too much ethnographic detail. In my view, superficial and simplified accounts of other cultures are patronizing and also inaccurate because they omit so much cultural depth. Lugbara culture, however poor the people themselves were in the material wealth on which the West sets such store, was one of honor, of generosity, and in a very real way of sophistication. It regarded people as thinking, feeling, and responsible human beings, with subtle rules and conventions about gentle behavior and respect toward one another and toward their environment. The underlying social organization of Lugbara society was complex—certainly equal in that respect to others anywhere—and it requires attention for a reader to understand it. But the attention does lead to understanding, whereas superficial accounts lead to nothing but easy condescension and even scorn for "The Other." There is enough of this in the world and I have no wish to contribute to it.

My relationship with those who accepted me as their guest, missing in the original account, was included in *The Study of the Lugbara* (1970b). Some anthropologists and non-anthropologists who seem to have little idea of what ethnographic research actually comprises have made a great deal of fuss about the writing and "inventions" of ethnography. Obviously, one may criticize the ethnographies of others without oneself being an ethnographer. But it would seem necessary at least to understand the professed aims and methods of ethnography as these have developed over time; those of the past are not those of today. Recent critics who see ethnography as a form of tourism, voyeurism, or as a way of inventing derogatory attributes of "The Other," show merely a myopic ignorance or unwillingness to understand the historical context of what has been written. It is easy to argue against a strawman, harder to understand the aims and methods of others. Those of my generation always understood (even if it seemed too obvious to spell it out in everything we wrote) that ethnographic research was a joint and equal task with those we lived among. All that I learned was shown to me by the Lugbara themselves, who decided what I should and could learn and what should not be shown to me, so the ethnographic research was a communal one. I alone wrote about them and so my interpretations are those presented in this book for both Lugbara and non-Lugbara readers: this book and some papers have been translated locally into the Lugbara language. I knew much less about their world than they did, and I was dependent upon them for insights, cultural emphases, and doors to understanding. But an ethnographer is not a mere scribe. As an ethnographer, I had been trained to perceive structural—and so unconscious—interrelations between acts and symbols that permit meaningful interpretation; that has been my role.

The aim of the ethnographer lies in the process of translation. He or she is not a traveler, nor a social adviser or development engineer out to change, destroy, or renew the culture of his or her hosts. Translation was the only task that my hosts could not do. It may naively be argued that this task is one of the exercise of power over others. But all social interaction involves power, as both I and the Lugbara knew very well. What matters is the way in which it is used, and I have tried to do what the Lugbara asked me to do, to help make known for their children and others their unique culture, of which they were rightly proud.

It is virtually—perhaps completely—impossible for any single way of life to be represented in its totality of "fact"; I have tried merely to evoke that way of life as it was at mid-century. I have tried to perceive the Lugbara world as they told me that they did, perhaps an impossible aim but not an unworthy one. If this revised edition is of interest to the Lugbara people of today, to whose parents and grandparents I owe so much, I shall be satisfied that I have done something of what they and I wished to do when we talked about their life during the years I was with them.

JM
Frankfurt am Main 1992

# Contents

*For M.G.*

CASE STUDIES IN CULTURAL

ANTHROPOLOGY

SERIES EDITORS

George and Louise Spindler

STANFORD UNIVERSITY

---

# THE LUGBARA OF UGANDA

Second Edition

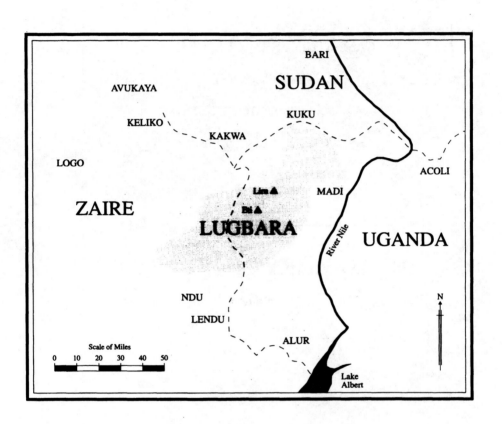

# 1 / The People and Their Country

## THE COUNTRY

During the period of my field research the Lugbara lived in the West Nile district of Uganda and in the Territoire de Mahagi of the then Republic of the Congo (Leopoldville). In 1948, the time of the previous census, there were 183,000 Lugbara in Uganda, 160,800 of whom lived in the West Nile district; the remainder consisted of labor migrants working or settled in various parts of southern Uganda (mainly in Bunyoro, Buganda, and Busoga). Congo figures for 1949 gave 58,200 Lugbara in that territory and some 2,500 Congolese Lugbara working in southern Uganda. There were also about 500 Lugbara in the Yei district of the southern Sudan. The Lugbara thus numbered in all about 242,000. In this book I shall deal only with the Uganda Lugbara as they were in their home district of West Nile, with references to changes that have been reported since then.

— The Lugbara are a Sudanic-speaking people. Linguistically their nearest neighbors are the Madi to their east and the Keliko and Logo to their west. Lugbara know of the Madi, Keliko, and Logo as being especially closely related to them, and their languages are mutually intelligible. Lugbara, Madi, and Logo were "like brothers" long ago, while the Keliko are said by Lugbara to be descended from a Logo man who married a daughter of one of the founding ancestors of the Lugbara people. To the north are the Nilo-Hamitic-speaking Kakwa and Kuku, who are also said to be descended from the same founding ancestors, and many of whose clans have the same names as do Lugbara clans. Culturally, if not linguistically, all these peoples are alike. To the south are the Nilotic-speaking Alur, and the Sudanic-speaking Ndu and 'Bale. Lugbara tell myths of the relationships between all these peoples and themselves, although not all are myths of origin. Some, as in the case of the ethnically unrelated Alur, merely give reasons for the two peoples being contiguous and hostile.

These peoples have usually been called "tribes," but this does not mean that they are very clearly defined units, nor are they single political entities. They are rather clusters of people who recognize themselves as being culturally distinct from their neighbors. Many of them share the same clan names and may intermarry; people living near the boundaries usually speak their neighbors' languages. Nonetheless, there is never any question as to where the boundaries lie, although, of course, these may change in time because of population movements and migrations.

1

The Lugbara live mainly along the line of the Nile-Congo divide, which at this point is also the political boundary between Uganda and Zaire. The divide rises from just under 4,000 feet above sea level in the north, where Uganda, Zaire, and Sudan meet, to over 6,000 feet in the south; most Lugbara live between 4,000 and 5,000 feet above sea level. They extend eastward to the escarpment that divides the highland region of the watershed from the wooded lowlands of the Nile valley, less than 2,500 feet above sea level. The lowlands are occupied by the Madi, although some small Lugbara groups spill over into them. In the north the escarpment ceases and the Lugbara extend to the Sudan border over the low-lying Aringa plains. To the west there is a broken escarpment that forms the boundary between the Lugbara and Keliko, beyond whom are the kingdoms of the Mangbetu and the Azande. To the south lies Alurland—high, broken country at the northern end of Lake Albert.

The Lugbara highlands are clearly marked off from the surrounding areas and are very distinctive. Almost all of Lugbaraland, except for the bush-covered area of Aringa in the north, consists of open, almost treeless, and densely cultivated rolling plains. Every mile or so there are small permanent streams and rivers, flowing into either the Nile to the east or one of the tributaries of the Uele to the west. Between streams are small hogsbacks, row upon row receding into the distance, many at that time crowned with clumps of eucalyptus or cassia trees but otherwise almost unwooded. Unlike most tropical African bush country, this area is green and fertile. Across the open country one can see for vast distances, except in the dry season from December to March, when there is too much haze. In the center of the country rise the two great masses of Mounts Eti (Wati on most maps) and Liru. On the southern borders stand Mount Luku and a string of smaller hills that form part of the Madi escarpment. These mountains are visible from every part of Lugbaraland in clear weather and have a conspicuous place in Lugbara mythology. The heart of Lugbaraland is the plateau bounded by the watershed and the circle of mountains Liru, Eti, and Luku. On it the Lugbara had lived largely isolated from their neighbors and the outside world.

## CONTACT WITH THE OUTSIDE WORLD

The "history" of a people such as the Lugbara were in the 1950s, when I lived among them, has been far more complex than often is simplistically held by historians and anthropologists today. Virtually nothing is known of them, in a documentary sense, before the advent of the first Arabs and Europeans who visited them in the late nineteenth century, most of whom left without leaving any written records. We know of the great rinderpest, meningitis, and other human and livestock epidemics in the 1880s and 1890s; we know that Arab slave raiding was endemic in the region throughout the nineteenth century and earlier; we know of the travels of Schweinfurth, Emin Pasha, Casati, Stanley and others in the second half of the nineteenth century, even though few of them actually did more than skirt the boundaries of Lugbara country. We may surmise an everlasting succession of epidemics, droughts, famines, and population movements going back for centuries. But we have no detailed knowledge of how these events affected the people or cluster of peoples that came to define themselves and so form a society that they called "Lugbara" during the first part of the twentieth century. Our knowledge goes back to only the remembered knowledge of some five or six generations from the time I worked there, to perhaps the 1870s at the earliest.

The Lugbara have been administered sporadically since 1900. At that time this area to the west of the Nile was part of the Lado Enclave, which had been leased in 1894 by the British to the Etat Independent du Congo. By 1885 Egyptian stations had been established among both the Kakwa and the Keliko and at several points along the Nile, but there were none in Lugbara. Emin Pasha stayed at Wadelai on the Nile from 1885 to 1889 and had a Lugbara servant and several Lugbara porters (some of whom were still alive in 1952), but he did not penetrate the distant highlands. The northern Lugbara spoke of four parties of Arabs who entered their country before the Belgians came in 1900, some of whom had contact with the more important Lugbara men. But the Lugbara were never seriously troubled by outsiders except on the northern and eastern borders of their country, and they escaped the terrible fate that met most of the small groups of the southern Sudan at the hands of Egyptian and Sudanese slavers.

It seems generally to be accepted by Western anthropologists and historians that the colonial impact was a cataclysmic event that happened at a particular date in history. In fact, it was nothing of the sort. It began with the appearance of a few European travelers who were associated in various ways with the Egyptian adminis- tration of the Sudan or the Belgian administration of the Congo Free State, many of whom were remembered as individuals in the oral traditions of Lugbara elders of the 1950s. Their impact was slight and it is their symbolic attributes of "invaders" from the "wilderness" that were recalled. The earliest Belgian administrators, those of the Sudanese interregnum, and the earliest British administrators after 1914, were all recalled in similar terms. In 1900 the Belgians began to administer the region, opening several posts, of which one, at Ofude, to the west of Mount Eti, was in Lugbara country. Ofude was occupied for five or six years and the garrison then withdrawn. There were four or five European officers, who rarely left the shelter of the encampment, and a detachment of Congo African troops. Relations were generally hostile and there was much raiding for cattle and grain by the troops. The Ofude Lugbara still told of the brutality and thieving tricks of the soldiers, aided by some of the Lugbara lineage heads and wealthier men whom the Belgians made *Makoto* ("chiefs"). Their rule was lightened by the excitement of raiding the post and shooting arrows at its occupants by night, but Lugbara speak of this regime as one that did nothing but bring them troubles.

The Belgian administration introduced agents or "chiefs" with wider powers than any that had existed in the indigenous society. These men had been the followers of a prophet, Rembe, a Kakwa living about forty miles north of Lugbara. He had dispensed sacred water in an effort to relieve the area of cerebro-spinal meningitis, rinderpest, Arabs, and Europeans; because all four calamities appeared at the same time they were causally interconnected in Lugbara thought. These men had all been important men before Rembe, and when the Belgians asked for the leading men of authority they came forward. As members of a cult meant to control European power they seemed the obvious persons to deal with the Belgians. They were made chiefs and paid for their services in cattle, thus being made rich beyond all Lugbara notions. Lugbara said that it was these men who first began to "spoil the land" and were responsible for so much of the trouble that had since befallen them. The Europeans and their troops came from outside the social system and were at first not assimilated into it; they behaved badly but then they merely behaved as Europeans and soldiers always did. In fact the Belgians are remembered as kindly men who spent most of their time "drinking gin and tea." The "chiefs," who were the people directly responsible for collecting levies, abused their traditional powers, forgot their traditional responsibilities to the people, and behaved in an upstart and greedy manner. It was toward them that most hostility was directed. It is significant that the word generally used to refer to Europeans, *Mandu* ("rifle"), also referred to chiefs and other Africans employed in the colonial administration. It meant essentially a person whose position was ultimately supported by government power.

In 1908, after the death of King Léopold II of the Belgians, the area became part of the Sudan. The effect was slight, although labor service and taxes were introduced over small areas. The Lugbara say that "work and rupees" were their lot in those years. It was at this time that the area became the scene of elephant-poaching on an immense scale, with ivory being taken by traders of all nationalities and without supervision or control; there was doubtless much effect on Lugbara daily life, but it is no longer possible to discover details.

In 1914 the southern portion of the Lado Enclave passed to Uganda, and A. E. Weatherhead took over the administration of the "New Areas," building a station at Arua, the present headquarters. Aru station in western Lugbara, which had never been part of the enclave and so had always been in the Congo proper, was opened about the same time, and the first shopkeepers, Arab and Indian, appeared. Weatherhead was still remembered vividly by the Lugbara, who described his appearance and behavior in detail. "He was a little man but very fierce, and walked among us without guns," it was said. He waged continual force against Lugbara groups for the first few years, as his early reports show, to "persuade" them to send representatives to Arua. He referred to the Lugbara as "wild and untractable," and as "shy and unorganized," requiring "severe measures" before submitting to administration.

The British administration began to affect everyday life by marking the Lugbara and other groups off from each other by gazetted boundaries, by introducing taxation, labor migration, consumer goods, education, Christianity, and the opportunities for a few political leaders to become wealthy and powerful under British protection. The slow effects of these factors had become qualititatively significant by the start of the Second World War. Radical structural changes took place elsewhere in East Africa much earlier—the coast during the eighteenth and nineteenth centuries, central Kenya and southern Uganda by the 1920s. Among the Lugbara and their neighbors—Madi, Alur, Kakwa, and others—these changes were slower and later, and among most of them were still not deeply felt until the horrors of Amin and Obote in the 1960s.

During the First World War, taxation was started and consumer goods were introduced by traders. In addition, cerebro-spinal meningitis, smallpox, and later

Spanish influenza, appeared, together with outbreaks of rinderpest—and the Kakwa prophet Rembe returned. He taught that the drinking of his sacred water would drive out disease and Europeans and bring back the Africans' cattle and dead ancestors. He also temporarily introduced a new form of organization to Lugbara. The cult was known as *Yakan,* or the "Allah water cult." Its activity culminated in a rising at Udupi in 1919, after which most of the Belgian-appointed chiefs, who had been reappointed by Weatherhead, were found to have been involved and were arrested and deported.

Weatherhead appointed "native agents," mostly Sudanese from the remnants of Emin Pasha's troops who had settled in various parts of Uganda. They maintained liaison between the district commissioner, the chiefs, and the local population, and were not withdrawn from the West Nile district until the mid-1920s. Since then, local administration had been in the hands of the chiefs. In the West Nile district (which included the Alur, Madi, and Kakwa, as well as the Lugbara) there were in the 1950s five Lugbara county chiefs (*opi* or *sultan*), each with about five subcounty chiefs (*wakil* or *joago*) under him. Under these were parish chiefs *(mukungu)* and village headmen *(nyapara).* Only these last two were representative of any indigenous groupings. Chiefs' councils were instituted in 1948 and represented clan and lineage groups as well as factional interests such as local Christians and Muslims. These posts were elective by popular vote, and there was also a superior district administration, in which posts were open to all peoples of the district. In the then Congo there was a similar organization, with five *makoto,* four of whom had very small chiefdoms and one of whom had a large territory and was the most important of all the Lugbara chiefs. Under them were *okils,* and under them *kapita* or headmen.

With the independence of both territories, much more stress was laid upon elections, and branches of the main political parties appeared. The Uganda Lugbara were strong supporters of the Uganda Democratic Party, which provided the first self-governing administration of the country. The Congo Lugbara were supporters of the late Patrice Lumumba.

Missions—the Africa Inland Mission (Protestant) and the Verona Fathers (Catholic)—entered the area in the 1920s, the former from the Congo and the latter from the Sudan. They had many small bush schools and several larger stations with European staffs. It is difficult to assess their influence, and indeed it cannot be considered apart from that of general European contact. Lugbara regarded missionaries as *Mundu* and saw them as agents of the power of the government that was in many ways antagonistic to the traditional systems of authority. Attendance at schools varied considerably from one area to another, and most children left school after only two or three years. But the general effect of the missions without doubt was very great, for they acted as a channel through which European ideas and objects were introduced to the people, as well as providing new religious and moral notions. Perhaps most important was their role as the only source of Western education, indispensable to anyone who wished to enter the modern power system of Uganda. Most Christians practiced both some form of Christianity and many traditional rites, and found little difficulty in reconciling them. They were significant in different situations, and it can be said that for all but a minority of Lugbara their traditional religious and moral beliefs were still accepted and the rites associated with them still practiced.

There were also several thousand Muslim Lugbara. Arua Town had a population of three thousand so-called Nubis, said to be the descendants of Emin Pasha's troops, but the term applied to any recently converted Lugbara man or a Lugbara woman who married a Nubi. Their role as traders and hawkers had given them an important economic position in the district.

In the 1950s, Lugbara still carried on their traditional way of life much as they had always done, and considered the outside world as something quite distinct from their own. Even though since the Second World War the effects of labor migration and of economic and political development schemes had become marked, for most of the adult population the government, whether European or that of an independent Uganda, was still extraneous and strange, existing for some purpose of its own. All old men remembered the pre-European era from their youth, and had taken part in feuding and warfare. The proportion of Lugbara women who had never seen a European was still very high, and those who had ever heard one speak or seen one closely were only two or three in a hundred. When young Lugbara men went as labor migrants to the south they behaved as members of that society in which they temporarily lived. When they returned to their homes they relapsed into the expected mode of behavior of young Lugbara adults.

## EVERYDAY LIFE IN THE 1950s

In this book I offer an account of how the Lugbara were when I lived among them in the early 1950s, a generation or more ago. I have written something of how I lived and worked at the time in another book and need not here repeat that account. But it is often difficult to gain a clear idea of the everyday life of another people; the cultural expressions of respect, affection, anger, ambition, grief, and envy, to name only a few basic emotions, may take very different forms, despite the general similarities of behavior among all human cultures.

Societies do not exist in a vacuum and we need to place the Lugbara of the 1950s within their temporal and spatial contexts. The most obvious factor to consider first is that they were then administered by the colonial governments of Britain (Uganda) and Belgium (the then Congo), whose policies and practices were very different. In Uganda all Lugbara under the age of thirty-five had lived under British administration all their lives; those older had experienced also the pre-British era when there had been virtually no centralized administration at all. Questions as to the morality of colonial rule hardly affected them: it was a fact to be accepted as part of the world in which they lived. Lugbaraland was remote from centers of government and the West Nile District of Uganda was literally closed to unauthorized visitors. During my stay there were seven British officials responsible for the district of some half million Africans, half a dozen Protestant and a dozen Catholic missionaries, a dozen Indian shops, one Indian labor recruiter, and three British tobacco growers and buyers. There was virtually no direct contact with

European officials, who relied upon local appointed chiefs to represent them to the people and the people to them. The establishment of a bureaucracy of chiefs and subchiefs was part of the establishment of a new system of law outside indigenous jural mechanisms; it also changed patterns of wealth and status in what had been basically an egalitarian society. The growth of markets had been important. They had appeared in Lugbaraland only since 1925 or so, and most of the traders in them were women exchanging small local surpluses for maize used in beer brewing. Markets were also places for distribution of cash and petty consumer goods, and the small traders who had opened shops near subchiefs' headquarters played similar roles.

A significant part of everyday life was a general sense of peace, security, and even prosperity, not in terms of comparison with other societies but in comparison with a turbulent past. The end of the last century and the early years of this had been times of incessant raiding, warfare, epidemics, and famines; since then these had virtually ceased. The colonial government, whatever its part in a wider history of exploitation, had stopped local warfare, organized famine relief centers, introduced medical services and a fairly efficient system of law, built roads, and introduced markets and peaceful forms of exchange. These were the developments that Lugbara themselves perceived as directly affecting them, not the long economic exploitation by exporting crops and labor for little return and the stultification of political progress and change. The grass-roots view was very different from that of national politicians, and the Lugbara feared those far more than they did the government officials at Arua Town. Members of the society lived in what they perceived to be some stability and order, however recent in history and however fragile in the face of the future.

What part did the Lugbara play in the wider societies of Uganda and the Belgian Congo in the years leading to the 1950s? Their main role was economic, providing certain cash crops, mainly tobacco and cotton. The difficulty was in their physical remoteness from larger centers—Kampala in Uganda, Stanleyville (Kisangani) in the Congo, and Juba in the Sudan—so that only very highly priced crops could profitably be exported. Tobacco was the most important, bought and cured in the district by an expatriate company. Lugbara exported their labor to the south, as sharecroppers to Nyoro and Ganda landowners and to Indian-owned sugar plantations and factories. They also provided much unskilled labor in Buganda and were recruited into the Uganda police and army. However, their remote position, the unattractiveness of their country to non-Lugbara, their general lack of modern education, their self-contained prosperity in their terms despite their poverty contrasted to other Ugandan peoples, and their general desire to avoid being drawn into the wider world, all meant that they played little part in the developing political economy of eastern Africa. They produced virtually no national political, religious, or cultural leaders, and appeared little affected by modern notions of ambition for wealth and power beyond local small-scale positions. Those with wider ambitions left the district, but few profited since wealth outside it was in the hands of BaGanda and BaNyoro, who regarded the Lugbara as little more than savages. It was not until later, under Idi Amin, that Lugbaraland was drawn into the national scene.

During my stay among the Lugbara they were virtually all peasant farmers, living in a fertile country that usually enabled them to produce adequate food and some items for sale. They had a reputation of being aggressive and quarrelsome people, and certainly they took as little notice as possible of the Ugandan and European agents of the governments of Uganda and the then Congo. I found them to be independent, very hardworking, generous and warmhearted to anyone who did not try to tell them what they should do. They had immense pride in their identity and their own abilities, and with good reason: their children were well fed and good mannered, even though they were desperately poor by Western standards. The commonest sounds one heard were those of human talk and laughter.

The Lugbara day began at sunrise, always about 6 A.M. throughout the year. The country is high and cold at night, but people had to rise at that time to get the day's work done. Women prepared food from the leavings of the previous evening's meal, children started taking livestock to pasture or prepared for the walk to the few "bush" schools run by the Christian missions around the district. Men set off for the fields, the beerhouses, or to take part in funerals, ancestral sacrifices, or oracular sessions. But the scale of daily movement remained small, rarely more than four or five miles. Before any of these activities people would wash in water laboriously carried from nearby streams, or would go themselves to the streams (Lugbara washed at least three times daily if they could). At that time women mostly wore carefully trimmed pubic leaves that were typically renewed at least once a day as they became dry and uncomfortable. Many younger women occasionally wore short pieces of imported cloth as skirts and men usually wore some form of shorts and shirts, although some older men retained their garb of animal skins. Most children went naked until they were five or six. Adults of both sexes had their lower incisors removed and their foreheads marked with rows of cicatrizations; girls and women had elaborate bodily cicatrizations also, as well as wearing beads, metal earrings, and lip plugs. Everyone used certain imported goods: matches, kerosene, cigarettes, beads, tea, salt, sugar, iron hoes, and small lengths of cloth were the most in demand and bought at weekly local markets from itinerant traders, or from the occasional local shops.

The homestead was a compound some twenty feet across in which were the house of the wife—a round building with mud and wattle walls and a thatched roof—and her granaries. A house had a single doorway, closed at night; only a few houses had window spaces. Inside was a bed of sticks and rushes, pegs for hanging possessions, and small alcoves in the walls for tobacco, matches, and other small objects. Most houses and compounds were kept clean by regular application of mud and cow dung, smooth and hard, and house walls were painted with lime wash and decorative patterns of ochre and soot (white, red, and black are the three Lugbara colors). Most compounds were fenced with thorn and euphorbia. The outside gate was closed at night, small animals kept inside and cattle in nearby byres. Around the compound were small rubbish dumps on which would be grown a few gourds and other useful plants and flowers. The compound was surrounded by others of the lineage, they in turn by irrigated and fertilized fields, and further beyond by larger fields under shifting cultivation. Always nearby were outcrops of granite on which women laid clothes to dry, and pounded grains and root crops.

During the daytime doors were never closed; theft was virtually unknown.

*A wife preparing millet porridge, the traditional staple.*

Houses, compounds, fields, and paths were all scenes of continuous work and talk. Even men drinking in beerhouses (where beer was sold by women entrepreneurs for a few cents a calabash) were considered to be working, as they were controlling local affairs and settling local disputes. But at the hoeing, planting, and harvesting seasons men performed the extremely hard work of cultivation; women were responsible for the continuous work of weeding, fetching firewood and water, and preparing food. There was little time in a day for resting, except for brief dozes by people who both worked very hard and who also suffered widely from anemia and other debilitating conditions. Giving orders and organizing the daily activities of others were thought ill mannered and unnecessary: everyone of the same age and sex did the same tasks, and all could see their lives and those of their children stretching ahead in certainty and a fair degree of contentment. There were few distinctions of wealth, which was mostly in the form of livestock used for marriages and sacrifice, and so accumulated in quantities only with difficulty and suspicion.

Regular occurrences were funerals and sacrifices, attended by both men and women. On moonlit evenings there were courtship dances that drew people from a wide area, with young men vying to attract unmarried women who danced with glistening skins and with flowers in their hair. By most evenings people were returning home to eat and talk. I recall vividly the wide evening landscape dotted with plumes of smoke from hundreds of cooking fires, the songs of women as they trudged home from washing and fetching water, and the tinkling of the bells tied around the necks of livestock. Except when there were dances, an hour or so after

*A woman and her children making string from sorghum stalks.*

dark all was silent except for lovers' meeting in the "girls' houses" attached to the larger compounds, and the occasional cries of drunken men returning home late.

Underlying the smiles and laughter, and the sudden outbursts of quarrelling, lay a complex pattern of organization seen by the people in terms of "respect" *(ru)*: Young respected old (or at least obeyed them), and women respected men of their own age or more; any younger man trying to tell a woman what to do would be ignored, laughed at, or sharply snubbed—and Lugbara women's vituperation, involving caustic and obscene sarcasm, was something to be avoided. The converse of "respect", a sentiment expressed in orderly and peaceful behavior, was envy or indignation, *ole*, expressed in competition and in witchcraft. *Ru* and *ole* were words heard continually in conversation, and I discuss them later.

## THE ECONOMY OF LUGBARALAND

Lugbaraland is a plateau that is divided into low ridges by the many small streams that thread their way across it. The tops of these ridges are often denuded of soil, exposing the grey granitic outcrops used as drying platforms for grain and cassava. The total soil depth is seldom greater than four feet, and although the soils vary considerably within Lugbaraland there are few parts with really poor soil. The rainfall is plentiful, averaging fifty-four inches a year. It is fairly evenly distributed, and except for the dry season from December to early March there are no periods without rain. August is the month of highest rainfall, although the rains that are important in the agricultural cycle are those that fall in March–April and October–November. Seasonal differences are not considerable enough to lead to transhumance or to have any marked effect on social life, except that in the dry season there is little work to be done in the fields, and beer and food are more plentiful after the main harvest period of July–August than at other times. Formerly there were periodic famines at the end of the dry season, recurring every ten years or so, which can be dated by the marriages of "cheap" wives who fled from famine areas and were married in return for shelter. Almost any genealogy will include one or two of these women. The last famine had been in 1942–1943, and since then the compulsory planting of cassava and the setting up of reserves of eleusine at subchiefs' headquarters had reduced the chances of others in the future.

The density of population was high for African subsistence farming. In parts of central Lugbaraland there were 250 people to the square mile; in the less fertile northern and western areas the figure was only 20, and the average for all Lugbaraland was about 150 to the square mile.

The Lugbara are predominantly cultivators, although cattle, goats, sheep, and fowl are kept in most areas. The varieties of crops grown and methods of farming

*Women catching flying ants as they swarm. Clay tubes are placed over a place of ants, and sticks are beaten to imitate rain. The ants swarm along the tube and fall into waiting pots. When cooked they taste like oatmeal.*

vary with differences in climate and soil types. The traditional crops are eleusine (the staple), sorghum, simsim, various peas and beans, groundnuts, pumpkins, sugar cane, bananas, and many other plants. After the 1942–1943 famine it had been compulsory for every man to grow a field of cassava, and in the 1950s this was becoming the staple; it is an easy crop to grow for a woman whose husband is away on labor migration, as it can be stored in the ground and has a high yield. Much maize was grown, mainly for beer making. Lugbara cannot grow cotton except in the eastern part of their country, as other areas are too high for it. A good deal of tobacco was grown for cash in the 1950s.

Meat and milk were unimportant in diet; fowl was eaten, but eggs were given only to infants, because it was thought that adults might become sterile by eating them. Game was no longer found in most of the highlands, but was plentiful in the Madi lowlands and the plains of northern Lugbaraland. Fish were found in streams and caught by nets. Ants were an important article of diet; the sound of women and children beating for ants was heard every evening at the beginning of the rainy season. Many wild herbs and fruit were gathered, the most important of which was shea butter nut.

Iron was smelted by Ndu smiths, and only rarely by Lugbara. The main source of iron was formerly in Zaire. It was usually obtained by Ndu themselves or by small parties of Lugbara. It would seem that the amount of iron in the form of artifacts that could be resmithed when required had been almost adequate for local

*Blacksmiths. They are not Lugbara but Ndu, a small ethnic group who practiced as blacksmiths in this region. They were endogamous and were greatly feared for their magical skills.*

needs. Expeditions were made to obtain the rough lumps of ore called *unzi,* which were used as bridewealth before the use of cattle for this purpose. Iron hoes were imported and when worn out were used as raw material by the smiths, scattered across Lugbaraland. Clay for pots, wood, ocher, chalk for whitewash, materials for basket-making, and the few other natural products used in traditional Lugbara economy were all obtainable locally over most of the country. Where they were not, as in the case of papyrus for matting, which was found in only a few remote places, they were obtained by parties of women. Such resources were not claimed by the people living near them. Others could collect them if they desired, although relations of personal friendship played some part. Oracle poisons from the Congo and rainstones from the Sudan were collected by men. Blood brotherhood was unknown, but people traveled great distances by invoking indirect ties of kinship. In this way they were given hospitality and protection.

Although there had always been a certain amount of traveling and trading across intergroup boundaries, for special commodities, everyday traditional requirements could be satisfied locally within a small neighborhood. It was thus possible for a very small territorial group to exist economically with only very slight recourse to external trading. There was also little specialization. Smiths, women potters, and occasional woodcarvers were the only specialists in material artifacts and could usually obtain raw materials in the neighborhood of their own homes. Other household articles of a traditional kind were made by the women as they wanted them. Apart from modern consumer goods imported from outside Uganda, the objects from outside the area were few.

There is little ecological difference between the various parts of Lugbaraland as

*A market in central Lugbara with women selling papyrus matting.*

*A market, with the wives of a single lineage sitting in a line displaying baskets of grain and legumes.*

far as traditional crops and materials are concerned, and there were no markets for local exchange before about 1925. During my stay there were markets at all subcounty chiefs' headquarters, with a large trade in foodstuffs and exchange of small local surpluses. This was centered around the growing of maize for beer brewing, the staple cottage industry. Maize was introduced into the area about 1925. Before then, beer was made of millet only, but maize has ousted millet as the popular material. Beer brewing was the only family occupation that could not be planned in advance and so catered for by seasonal planting, because the drinking of beer was an essential concomitant of all rites and ceremonies, as well as of visiting between kin and friends. Formerly households were larger, and the need for beer millet could normally be met from within the household. This pattern became less common, and trade in maize was therefore necessary for every family. Trading was also done in markets for soap, tobacco, kerosene, and other goods, as well as for pots, grinding stones of granite, papyrus mats, and other articles made by energetic and skillful women, although any woman could make these things if she wished. Most imported articles were sold at the few African shops in the smaller rural townships and at Indian and Arab stores at the one or two larger centers. African shopkeepers also set up stalls in markets in their area. Besides dealing in trade goods they acted as distributors of cash and gave credit, and were thus more than mere petty shopkeepers. Most of these little shops had a sewing machine for making clothes, and some of them had lorries in which they collected small surpluses of export crops and thereby acted as middlemen between the peasant producers and the larger Indian traders in the towns.

In the past Lugbara had no currency, exchange being by barter. In recent years Lugbara became involved in the money economy of the rest of Uganda, with the introduction of taxation, in the Congo part in 1912 and the Uganda part in 1918, and the growth of a demand for consumer goods that could only be acquired for cash. The society was no longer economically self-sufficient. This process became marked after about 1925, when Lugbara began to go outside their own district to earn money. The rapid expansion of southern Uganda dates from that time, and the West Nile district and adjoining parts of Zaire and Sudan became peripheral areas supplying labor to the industries and plantations of the wealthy south. In 1951, out of a total Lugbara population of some 242,000, there were 14,000, or 5.7 percent, in the south. Most of these were men, about 20 percent of the adults being absent at any one time. The absentee rate varied from one area to another, due to several factors, of which the most important was land scarcity, there being a higher absentee rate in the densely occupied parts of central Lugbaraland than in other areas. The type of migration also varied. Some men went to work for wages on contract and returned after a year away; others went to settle and to grow their own cash crops in the south, which the Lugbara regarded from this point of view as an extension of their lands that could be used to make money. Many of the latter took their wives with them and eventually became "lost" to their kin.

## FARM AND SETTLEMENT

The first detailed account of Lugbaraland was written by the Sudan government officer in charge of the area in the years immediately after 1908. He was an acute observer, and wrote of Lugbara (Stigand 1925:19, 89):

> The country to the south (of Kajo Kaji) however, still remained in a disintegrated state; only a few of the chiefs, and those almost entirely at the north end of the country, have any number of followers, or authority. The rest of the tribe is split up under numberless petty chiefs, acknowledging no superior. . . . In 1912 I counted over one hundred so-called chiefs in the comparatively small area between the Koshi and the Alla rivers.

Here he was describing the northern Lugbara. Of central Lugbaraland he wrote:

> To the south of Wati (Mt. Eti) . . . there are an immense number of little communities, some under petty chiefs having only a few dozen followers, and some under no chiefs at all. These are mostly Lugware, but towards Mount Baker (Luku) they gradually merge

into Madi. The disorganization of this part of the country was so complete that it was absolutely unparalleled by anything I have seen elsewhere, or heard about. . . . On pitching camp near a village, people would come out and stand in a group about two hundred yards or more distant and watch proceedings. Every time anyone approached them, or shouted to them to come and speak to us, all would turn and fly, coming back later when they found that they were not followed. It was generally only on the second day that they became so bold as to come near enough to speak to, and not till the third day that one was able to buy food from them. As the community was very small, this meant only a few little baskets of flour. On moving to another village only a mile or two away, one would have to go through the whole of this exasperating game again, as there was seldom any communication between neighbouring villages. Each little group was perfectly isolated.

At the time Stigand traveled through the country only a small area below Mount Eti had been subjected to any degree of influence by the Belgian administration, and there had been a few years of ivory-poaching when the area had been virtually unadministered. Stigand thought that it had been disorganized by Arab slavers, but it is certain that they never penetrated this far. There is no reason to doubt that this description was substantially that of longstanding Lugbara society. This type of fragmentary organization seems in fact to have been typical of most of the small societies of the southwest Sudan and northeast Congo, except for the states of Zande and Mangbetu. In Uganda this type of organization was found only among the Lugbara and the Kakwa, although it would appear that the Madi also may at one time have had this kind of system (Middleton 1955).

Lugbara was a land of peasant cultivators, living at a high density of population. It was not bushland roamed by animals, but farmland filled with huts and fields. In the dry season and after the main harvesting, from August onward, the huts stood out in the landscape amid cleared fields. But while the crops were growing the compounds might be almost hidden in the dense crops—the larger varieties of sorghum are seven or eight feet high—and the appearance of the country was quite different. At this time there is rain and the atmosphere is clear, so that one can see great distances across the farms and settlements; but in the dry season there is much haze and one may not see more than a mile or two, and the land is no longer green but parched and dry. Homesteads were scattered across the ridges of this open upland country. The Lugbara were polygynous, although over 60 percent of the married men had only one wife, and each wife had her own hut, granaries, and fields. In the compound there were three granaries for a wife, one each for eleusine, sorghum, and legumes, and occasionally a woman had another for grains already mixed for beer brewing, and a small high granary for groundnuts. In a polygynous household the husband might have a hut for his own use, mainly for the entertainment of guests. The huts of one husband, with their granaries, typically formed a distinct compound, separate from other compounds of related men, and surrounded by its own hedge of euphorbia, climbing beans, pumpkins, and other plants. In the more recently settled areas in southern Lugbaraland, where the compounds of immigrants had become intermingled on the ground, each wife of a polygynous husband usually had her own hut in its own separate compound, away from those of her co-wives.

Physically the compound was the most distinctive unit, a cluster of huts and granaries standing alone, surrounded by its fields. The term used for it is *aku or 'buru*, referring to the floor of mud and dung kept clean by daily sweeping, and on which the everyday life of the women was conducted. There was usually only one entrance to the compound. Inside the compound were the dwelling huts and granaries, under which were the ghost and other shrines and magical plants. The three upright stones of the fireplace, the center of the women's activities, were placed in a sheltered corner of the compound floor. The word *lico* is often used to refer to large compounds, especially when talking of those of the past. *Lico* means literally "hedge" and is used for the circular hedge set around a compound or a cattle kraal, built near the homesteads and shared by several families of the same lineage. *Aku, 'buru,* and *lico* refer to a single residential settlement of any size, from a homestead containing the hut of one wife to that containing the huts of a family group of three or four generations. Besides the living huts there was sometimes an unwalled cooking hut or shelter, and in any group of related compounds there was usually a girls' hut where the unmarried girls slept with their lovers, and where guests might sleep also.

Lugbara recognized different types of ground: uncultivated land; ground left fallow for a few years; new fallow after cropping that had not yet regained its

*An old woman in her compound, lighting a pipe from a burning twig from the central fire.*

fertility; later fallow that showed by the presence of certain plants that its fertility had been restored and was again ready for hoeing; and newly cleared and hoed land that was being left for a few months before second hoeing and planting. All these had specific terms. Lugbara knew that different crops needed different soils and rotations. Crops were rarely grown in pure stands, each crop being grown with certain others. Those in a single field were chosen with regard to maintaining soil fertility and ease of harvesting—the crops ripened consecutively in the single field. The crop rotations depended on the nature of the crop varieties and other factors— variance in growing times, recognized fertilizing qualities (e.g., legumes and cassava, known to fertilize and clean a field), their ability to provide shed leaves as a mulch, and so on.

Each homestead, occupied by a single wife, had three types of fields: the *amvu akua* (fields at home), the *amvu amve* (fields outside), and the *yimile* (riverine or irrigated fields). The last had high fertility and were used for sweet potatoes, maize, sugar cane, and bananas, and were given very short fallow periods. They were irrigated by small channels cut to take water from a permanent stream running between two ridges. Home fields were fertilized with ashes and manure and were used for the more demanding crops, especially the white sorghums used in beer brewing. Outside fields were not fertilized and were used for the staple, eleusine, grown with sorghums, simsim, and pigeon pea. The rotation cycles were different for each type of field, and only the outside fields could be said ever to be under a system of shifting agriculture; the others were farmed permanently. Outside fields were traditionally cultivated for two or three years and then reverted to bush. They were usually opened after three years' fallow, but the length of fallow depended on soil fertility, and some fields might be left for as long as ten years. Home fields had a far higher proportion of cultivation to fallow. Some crops were also grown on the rubbish dumps outside the compounds, and on old hut sites, but these were outside the main agricultural system, as not all homesteads possessed them; they were used particularly for tobacco for home consumption (that for sale to tobacco traders was grown on home or outside fields). Fallow was used for grazing, and there were also specific grazing areas, usually where the soil was known to be too thin for permanent cultivation.

Generally, men opened and cleared the ground, which was the heavy work, and women weeded and harvested. Both men and women sowed, depending on the crop. Men also cleared the irrigation channels in the riverine fields. Once harvested, the crops belonged to the wives, who were responsible for their care and use, although men took the cash crops.

The riverine land was the kind that was traditionally scarce. In the past there was ample room for other types, but in recent years the outside farms have also disappeared. Nevertheless, the average amount of land needed for each wife had remained constant. Throughout Lugbaraland, despite all differences of crop type and rotation and agricultural methods, the average amount of land cultivated per head in 1953 was the same, between 2,400 and 2,500 square yards. Fields might be scattered, but rarely lay outside the boundaries of a settlement's traditional field area. This scattering was due to differences in soil type and water supplies. Generally, each wife had fields of all types and of equal fertility to those of other wives of the group. These requirements meant that there was a fairly fixed relation between the number of wives of the group and the extent of its territory. It meant also that there was a maximum size for a single farming group. Once a group's territory had no more of any single type of field within reasonable walking distance, any increase in the number of its wives might lead to the dispersal of its huts. It seems that typically the wives of up to twenty adult men could share a single stretch of land. In the case of some wives' finding it difficult to obtain all three types of land, the opposition between them led to quarreling and often to accusations of poisoning and other jealous behavior. A man with more than one wife prefered to put the various types of his wives' fields together, to make his work of clearing, burning, and hoeing easier and to avoid quarreling between his wives as to which one had been given the best land and had received the greatest and most careful labor. But men said that the wives still quarreled and preferred to have their plots separated. The husband usually had his way in this respect and this provided one of many rationalizations for the hostility of co-wives. It was as good a rationalization as any, but men grumbled over their beer gourds that in the end it all came back to women's natural propensity to quarrel among themselves and with their husbands.

There were, however, various ways in which shortage of a particular type of farmland could be overcome without splitting up the entire group. The traditional way was for single households to move. A man took up residence with a kinsman elsewhere, usually his wife's or mother's brother. Land shortage was not the only reason for such a move, but case histories show that it was the most common. Such tenants were usually young men who had just married and had no fields available for their new wives. A tenant might not be deprived of his rights over land, which were heritable, until he or his descendants decided to break the tie.

A young man might also go to southern Uganda to work as a laborer for Nyoro or Ganda landlords, for Indian or Ganda employers, or to grow cotton on his own account. This migration was in many ways a form of tenancy. The main reason was to gain cash, but the flow of migration from an area was affected by the degree of land shortage, the areas with the most shortage supplying the most migrants. A balance was established between the effective population (that is, the population wholly or mainly dependent upon the land for its livelihood) and the availability of farmland. By migrating outside their own country Lugbara were able to borrow and use the soil fertility and land of southern Uganda, and also lessen the land pressure in their own areas. By migrating temporarily the migrants did not break their ties with family and community, but solved the immediate problem of land scarcity: as they grew more senior in the lineage they could acquire land and then send their juniors in their turn.

Traditionally the huts of a residential group formed a single large compound, or perhaps a cluster of compounds with only a few yards of pathway, rubbish heaps and cattle compounds between them. Huts were clustered together and fields dispersed around the hut cluster. Each group had its home fields immediately adjoining it, the outside fields often being a mile or more away, and as much as ten miles in parts of eastern Lugbaraland where land was poor and uncrowded. The largest local group was the subtribe (which is described in a later chapter), averaging some four thousand people living in an area of up to twenty or so square miles. Compounds and home fields were in the center, on the tops of ridges with riverine fields in the valley bottoms between them; and around them were the outside fields and grazing areas. The subtribal territory was divided among component groups, each separated by its own belt of home fields, and occasionally by a stretch of outside fields as well.

This traditional system had changed almost everywhere by the 1950s. As soon as land became locally scarce three developments occurred. There might be a proliferation of tenants (including the labor migrants) as has already been described. Whole groups might move and settle elsewhere in empty land, but this was rare since there was little unused land except on the periphery of the country, and Lugbara did not like to move far, so that in the crowded center this course was not often taken. Or the type of farming would change. In much of central Lugbaraland outside fields had almost vanished, as had grazing grounds except in those parts where the soil was too thin to be used for cultivation. Crops that were grown formerly on outside fields were now grown on home fields, where crop rotations were lengthened to accommodate them. Areas formerly used as outside fields were now used for compounds and new home fields. This meant that the pattern of settlement had changed also. The former peripheral areas of outside fields were now occupied both by tenants from other groups and by members of the group itself, who had moved from the center of the territory to other parts of it. The traditional pattern of large hut clusters had changed to one of scattered homesteads, each belonging to the wives of a single man or set of brothers only. With such a pattern it was easier to assure a satisfactory distribution of fields between wives. In addition, this pattern permited a higher density of effective farming population. Another factor was polygyny. Lugbara said that formerly there had been more polygyny than there was in the 1950s, when 63 percent of married men had only one wife. This was clearly an opinion that could not be proved, due to lack of reliable evidence for the past, but if correct it provided a further reason for the dispersal of homesteads.

Government regulations also affected the pattern of settlement. Traditionally the distribution of Lugbara settlement was always in a state of slow change. The people say they came from the north or northwest and when the Europeans entered the country they were still drifting southward. There were no stable boundaries between local communities, and an expanding group could acquire control over an area at the expense of a contracting group. However, the government had fixed boundaries between subtribes at the places where these were when it created chiefs, and had tried to stabilize territorial movement. Men would still show where their fields, grazing grounds, and former village areas had been "before the Europeans came." There had also been a considerable increase in population. One consequence had been an ever-increasing disparity between the distribution of population and that of land, so that instead of the density of population varying according to the carrying capacity of the land of any one place, there was now serious maldistribution of population to land. The people of one community might be living at a far higher density than those of neighboring ones. Boundaries were fixed and people who attempted to move across them (as they would traditionally have done) were haled before a government chief as troublemakers. This affected the traditional process of dispersal of local settlements according to their land requirements. It led to an increase in the incidence of individual tenancy, because although a group could not cross a chiefdom boundary an individual tenant might do so if he had kin on the other side.

# 2 / The Form of Lugbara Society

## HIGH PEOPLE AND LOW PEOPLE

In this chapter I show how the Lugbara conceived of themselves and their own society. All people must be able to do this, but of course each people has its own way of doing it, due to varying historical, economic, political, and other circumstances that for a preliterate society may usually only be guessed at. Here I do not try to reconstruct the history of the Lugbara, but limit myself to what they told me about themsleves.

Most Lugbara did not know what the limits of their society were in space, except for those employed as government chiefs, clerks, police, former labor migrants, and refugees in the Sudan. But all knew that the people near and around them were Lugbara, and they could see for many miles across the open Lugbara plateau with the two mountain massifs of Eti and Liru standing in the center. These mountains are at the heart of Lugbara: not that they are in the exact center geographically—Liru is almost on the Kakwa border—but they are the focus of all myth and genealogy. Lugbara were aware that they did not live in isolation, but were members of a society whose land stretched for a great distance. All these people whose lands were visible were members of a single system, conceptually even if not politically so. Among the Logo to the west in the Congo, the Kakwa to the north in the Sudan, and the Acoli to the east of the Nile, people lived in small settlements that were surrounded by bush. Paths led away through the trees and grass to other settlements that were invisible. There was a sense of isolation and discreteness from them. These countries seemed to be almost empty of population by comparison to the densely occupied Lugbara highlands. In Lugbara one lived in a homestead from which one could see the surrounding ridges, each covered with huts and cultivation. One could see the members of neighboring families and lineages in their homes and fields. At night one could see the fires smoldering in their compounds and, in the grass-burning season, the lines of fires blazing in their fields. One was aware of belonging to a small group set in a system, which included all the other similar groups spread out across the open country stretching away on all sides to the distant territories of people unvisited and hostile, yet actually visible and thus easily conceived as belonging to one system. Some parts of Lugbara along the Congo-Uganda border were almost uninhabited, with a thick growth of secondary forest. This was often pointed out to me as being unlike what Lugbara country should be, and as a place to be feared. Compounds were set in open fields. It was only the strips of bush along the larger streams that remained the haunts of *adroanzi* ("the children of Spirit"), creatures to be feared and avoided.

At the center of the Lugbara world were the two mountains. They were the focus of Lugbara myths of creation, which were common to all Lugbara groups. Certain neighboring peoples, notably the Kakwa, were also featured in these myths, and were thus brought within the same social system. Lugbara and most of their neighbors could be regarded as a single congeries of peoples. Certainly "Lugbara society" was defined culturally in terms of slight cultural differences, of which the most important was the acceptance of the name "Lugbara," which has no literal meaning and may in any case be of fairly recent origin.

The Lugbara spoke two main dialects: *Uruleti* (high speech) and *Andraleti* (low speech). I refer to them as High Lugbara and Low Lugbara. The differences between them were marked. High Lugbara was close to Keliko and they were mutually intelligible, near the boundary at any rate, although High Lugbara was not so mutually intelligible with Logo, which was said to be so with Keliko. Low Lugbara was very close to Madi. Low Lugbara could not be understood by the Keliko, nor High Lugbara by the Madi, and it was not easy for High and Low Lugbara speakers to understand each other if they came from groups widely separated.

Although High and Low Lugbara were intelligible respectively with Keliko and Madi, the latter groups were not Lugbara. Lugbara recognized the close relationship, but there was never any doubt as to the boundary of Lugbaraland, of what I call Lugbara society. This boundary was marked physically by a thinly populated belt between the Lugbara and the neighboring peoples. But the principal distinction was a cultural one. There were minor differences in culture, mainly in material culture, within Lugbara. Huts, granaries, ornaments on baskets and gourds, tattoo marks, types of baskets, women's knives, and other features varied every few miles. With them went dialectal variations in pronunciation and vocabulary. These and similar differences were found throughout the Logo-Keliko-Lugbara-Madi belt of peoples. The boundaries of Lugbara were marked more by a coincidence of many variations than by any other factor, except that of their accepting the ethnic name Lugbara.

Lugbara said that the speakers of High Lugbara were the Urule'ba (High People), and those of Low Lugbara were the Andrale'ba (Low People). High and Low People were distinguished by linguistic differences in this sense: one could draw a line—although it would be an arbitrary one—on a map and say that to the west of it were High Lugbara and to the east Low Lugbara. But if we were to do this we would distort the significance of this division for the people themselves. It was by the concepts of High People and Low People that Lugbara comprehended their society and its position in the wider world. These concepts were focused on the two hero-ancestors, Jaki and Dribidu.

The hero-ancestors were associated with the mountains Liru and Eti. Every Lugbara group of any size had its own genealogy going back ultimately to one of these heroes. People said that the hero-ancestor of the High People was Jaki. This was an axiomatic statement: High People were defined by their being descended from Jaki and by speaking High Lugbara dialects, but the former criterion was the more important. Jaki was the son of Yeke, who lived somewhere to the north and was the third or fourth generation from Gborogboro, the first man on earth. Yeke married two wives, one being Gbele from Koboko in Kakwa, the mother of Jaki, and the other Ngada, the ancestor of the Kuku and Bari, according to Lugbara. High Lugbara were thus closely related to the Kakwa, Kuku, and Bari, and said that once they spoke the same language but it was forgotten after a "Tower of Babel" that reached to the sky fell down, and their ancestors then learned to speak Lugbara. Jaki came to Lugbara country and his doings and wanderings were associated with Mount Liru, on which he died.

Dribidu was the hero-ancestor of the Low People. He also came from the north, and was often said to be Jaki's brother, but whereas Jaki came directly to Mount Liru via what is now Kakwa country, Dribidu came via the Nile valley and wandered through eastern Lugbaraland. He was associated with Mount Eti, a few miles southeast of Liru. He died a few hundred yards below the main peak; what were said to be his grave, his hut-post holes, and his broken cooking pots were still visible there in 1950.

Lugbara related the wanderings and activities of the heroes at length and in immense detail. They had many sons, who were the founders of Lugbara clans. They were thus significant in being the focal points of relationships between local groups, and stories of their death on the mountains and their burial there were told whenever the relationship between clans was under discussion.

High and Low People were in no way divisions with political functions. But a High group had a sentiment of cultural, linguistic, and territorial closeness with other groups that its members considered also to be High People. The same situation was found among Low groups. These divisions were defined relatively. The west was associated wih High People and the east with Low People. The principle of definition was that those groups to one's west were usually High People and those to one's east were Low People. In addition, groups north and south, if far enough away to be beyond the range of everyday contact, were likely to be placed in the opposite division from oneself. A High Lugbara would wave his hand along the horizon and say, "Those people over there and those people over there are all Low People; it is we and these people near us here and the people to the west who are High People. But perhaps some others are High People also, who can know all these things?" Although definition was thus partly by social distance, geographical position was also important. If a group lived near the mountain associated with its division, all those groups living anywhere near the mountain would be said to be of the same division; but a group that was far from its mountain might well say that the people living near it belonged to the other group, because they were outside the range of immediate social relations. Groups that called themselves High People buried their dead with their heads in the direction of Liru, while Low People buried theirs with their heads in the direction of Eti.

Besides giving each group its place in the total society, this definition enabled Lugbara to place their society as a unit within the cluster of peoples of the region. Lugbara said that Keliko, Kakwa, and Logo were High People and that Madi were Low People. Lugbara were thus in the center of the cluster. I do not know whether Keliko or Kakwa themselves said that they were descended from Jaki, as Lugbara said they were, but some Madi groups did say that they spring from Dribidu. The peoples to the south, Alur, 'Bale, and Ndu, did not feature in this schematization.

Contact with them was recent and they were very different in culture. Lugbara society was oriented northwest, toward the peoples with whom they claimed a common ethnic origin.

We see here the operation of a common principle. All groups of a society could be related genealogically, by Lugbara ways of thinking. The more distant socially, the further back geneaologically was the tie that related them; the closer socially, the closer the genealogical link. Any Lugbara group knew only its own genealogies and something of those of its immediate neighbors, who were always considered to be of the same division. Beyond one's own community, little or nothing was known of the genealogies of other groups. Thus the division into High and Low People was a relative one, the distribution of which differed for every group in Lugbara. The historical past of another group's ancestry was irrelevant; what was relevant was its present territorial and social relationship to one's own. It was clear also that in this context social distance was equated more or less with spatial distance. The division into High and Low People was seen in territorial terms.

## MYTH, TIME, AND SPACE

Lugbara said they are descended from the first creatures put on earth by Spirit at the beginning of the world. Lugbara were all "of one blood" *(ari alo)*, created by Spirit the creator of men *(Adroa 'ba o'bapiri)*. Spirit created a man, Gborogboro, and a woman, Meme, and domestic livestock. Meme had wild animals in her womb. The gazelle broke out and was followed by the other beasts. After the animals had left Meme's womb Spirit put children in it, according to some versions; others say that she became pregnant after goat's blood has been poured over her legs;[1] still others say that the pair were taught how to have sexual intercourse, which was followed by conception. Meme bore a boy and a girl. Myths tell that these siblings produced another male and female pair, who did the same in their turn There were several generations of siblings, after which the heroes, Jaki and Dribidu, were born.

Other myths told of the separation of mankind from Spirit in the sky, the separation of "black" and "red" (European and Arab) peoples, the building of a Tower of Babel and its destruction, and the appearance of Lugbara and Kakwa and other diverse peoples and languages. All these events took place somewhere to the north of Lugbaraland. They were not related to each other nor put into any time sequence except insofar as the creation itself preceded all human activities.

This corpus of myth culminated in the two hero-ancestors coming to the present country of the Lugbara and there begetting sons who were the founders of the present clans. The heroes were not human as men are now. Dribidu means "the hairy one," since his body was covered with long hair. He was also known as 'Banyale ("eater of men"), since he ate his children until he was driven out of his earlier home. He came to the Lugbara highlands and there found a leper woman who gave him fire with which to cook his buffalo meat. He cured her with

---

[1]It was said that she did not menstruate. Lugbara believed that conception occurs only in the three or four days following menstruation, so that the pouring of blood "showed" her how to menstruate and, like menstruation, was followed by conception.

medicines, the secrets of which are now lost. He then made her his first wife (mothers of his previous children are irrelevant and so not known). He impregnated her, which resulted in feud with her kin and the subsequent payment of seduction fine and bridewealth. He did the same with other leper women, and after begetting many sons died on Mount Eti. Similar myths are told of Jaki.

The heroes were not normal human beings, living in a society and recognizing its values. They mark the appearance of Lugbara society in the form it had through the 1950s. The heroes married many women and their sons married wives and had children, thereby becoming the founders of clans. The latter-day groups were thus descended from the founders of the original clans, with continual proliferation and amalgamation. The ancestors who featured in these genealogies were always regarded as having been normal social beings who had behaved in a way that men did behave and believe they should behave—for the reason, of course, that the ancestors laid it down that they should. All special rights and mystical powers possessed by certain men of certain lineages—for example, the power to control the rain or to possess certain magical objects—were validated by their having originated at the time of the heroes or of their sons. For Lugbara, their society was essentially the same as it had been at that time.

The several accounts of the creation of the pairs of siblings, the hero-ancestors, and their descendants differed in character. The accounts of the creation and of the activities of the siblings before the heroes may be called mythical; those of the clan-founders' descendants may be called genealogical; those of the heroes themselves presented both mythical and genealogical features, that is, they may be placed in either category on different occasions. If we put them on a time scale, the heroes are either at the end of the mythical period or at the beginning of the genealogical period. But to do this is to distort the significance of these accounts. The difficulty is that Western myths and histories are placed on a time scale and therefore the concepts we use in this context contain a reference to nonrecurrent measured time.

The main difference between the period before the heroes and that after them (the heroes appearing in both periods) was that in the latter the personages were ordinary beings and clan members behaving in the way that people did normally, but in the former they behaved in a reverse manner and lived in social isolation in a world in which there were no clans. They committed incest, not yet recognizing ties of kinship; they did not transfer bridewealth for their mates, and ties of affinity and the family as such were not yet recognized; they could do marvelous feats that men can no longer achieve—the first pair of siblings were called Arube ("worker of miracles") and O'du ("miraculous omen"), and the other siblings had names associated with magic or the introduction of techniques by magical means; they were sometimes said to have been born with teeth. Their characteristics were nonhuman or contrahuman. It was with the appearance of the heroes and their begetting sons that human beings became social beings living in a society. Before that they were not members of a society—there was no society, in fact—and they and their world existed in the north outside present Lugbara territory, a territory where every part was associated in tradition with a particular clan. Before he entered Lugbaraland, Dribidu was a cannibal, eating his own children. Once arrived in Lugbaraland the heroes became more or less social beings, but always retained some superhuman and magical qualities. They learned the art of fire making from the leper women, whom they then turned from incomplete women (lepers) into complete and social women by curing and marrying them. I refer to the attributes of the preheroic figures as "inverted." Their inverted and superhuman attributes were indexes of their asocial existence before the formation of an ordered society.

A similar use of myth could be seen in the accounts of the appearance of Europeans in Lugbaraland. The ancestor of the "red" people was Angbau, the brother of Yeke, who was the father of Jaki, so that the red people had a parallel existence to the black people. But this was outside Lugbara society. Those Europeans who entered it were placed in a different category. Those who first came to Lugbaraland were called by various names, but they were all given similar attributes. They were cannibals (as all Europeans were thought to be until recently, except those well known as individuals), they could disappear underground, and they walked on their heads and could cover vast distances in a day by this means. As soon as they were noticed they began to walk on their legs, but if attacked they would vanish into the ground and come up some distance away. They would then move away on their heads. They were thus literally "inverted." I heard it said that this was still the way Europeans behaved in their own country "beyond Lake Albert." In 1900 the Belgians came. Myth said that when they came everyone ran away. The Belgians and their cruel and reputedly cannibalistic troops chased the fugitives and found one or two important men hiding in the bushland outside their homesteads; these men were made "chiefs" by the Belgians. Chiefs were often known as the "clients" (atibo) of the Europeans. Since the presence of clients in a homestead was always explained by saying that an ancestor found them "hiding in the grass" outside the homesteads and took them in as "his people," the appointment of chiefs was also explained in these terms. It is hardly necessary to add that in fact they did not run away nor were they found hiding, according to detailed accounts given to me by persons who were there in 1900.[2] Other accounts say that because the Europeans came from outside society, as clients in time of famine, they were taken in and welcomed by important men who acted toward them as "fathers": they were then made chiefs by the Europeans. It is clear that either version explained the way in which the Belgians and the new chiefs became part of Lugbara society. It was said that the first British administrator, A. E. Weatherhead, could walk across the country at fantastic speeds; no sooner was it thought that he was safely away a hundred miles to the north, and people began to attack his headquarters at Arua or to fight their neighbors, then he would suddenly appear in person among them. He was said to have had powers of personality, courage, and sympathy that could be due only to magic and heroic qualities. "His words were strong" and he impressed them as no other Europeans, before or after him, had ever done.

Since those days Europeans entering the country have had a place in Lugbara society and an expected role to play there. There were different categories of Europeans but they all had fixed statuses. Lugbara could list most of their district commissioners and missionaries since the days of Weatherhead. Other government

---

[2]Accounts of the head-walking Europeans were given to me by men who were eyewitnesses to their arrival. But the necessary use of the idiom of inversion to describe the concept of "asocial" was more meaningful to Lugbara than a dry photographic account.

officers were rarely remembered but it was thought that there was some kind of genealogical or quasi-genealogical tie between district commissioners and between missionaries. I often heard it surmised that certain Europeans were the sons or sisters' sons of earlier figures. But all these Europeans behaved in a normal way and had none of the superhuman qualities of Weatherhead.

For Lugbara, time was periodic, reckoned mainly by generations of men and women, the seasons, the stars, the moon, and the sun.[3] All these phenomena occurred at regular intervals and were not placed on a scale of nonreccurrent time. Events that did not recur were not put on a measured time scale. Lugbara myth and genealogy were little related to historical time. Genealogy explained and validated the social relations between living people. No Lugbara knew much of the genealogies of clans other than his or her own, since they were for the most part outside everyday experience. Genealogies dealt with social beings as members of a given community, and the ancestors were only significant, and therefore remembered, insofar as the relationships between them validated the present composition of the community. But the ancestors were placed in society, and society itself was given meaning and validity, by myth. Myths in Lugbara dealt with personages who originally were not members of society, beings whose relations with one another were asocial, in that they did not recognize the obligations of kinship and neighborhood. Most of the values and sanctions concerned with social behavior were associated with the cult of ancestral ghosts, and there was no ritual attached to the mythical figures. The myth themes ended with certain personages forming or entering the society and receiving a status within it. As the extent of the society increased and new persons were introduced into it, as had been the Europeans and their chiefs, they were given identity and status by means of myth. Mythical figures were outside society and genealogical figures were within it, and there were some personages—the heroes and the first district commissioner— who belonged to both myth and genealogical tradition. The two were thus linked and derived significance and validity from each other. But to set them into a scale of historical time is misleading, because the events were related to each other not by their temporal relationships but by the social and moral relationships between the personages whose activities composed the myth and genealogical tradition.

We put the events I have described in a scale of time. Similar concepts were used by the Lugbara to refer to a scale in space. The same thematic pattern, with normal members of society at the center, then a belt of quasi-members who possessed some superhuman and inverted attributes, and beyond them the remainder of the world peopled by inverted beings, could be discerned in Lugbara notions of the world as it was in the 1950s. The relations between people and groups within a local community were expressed and validated by genealogical tradition. Beyond the community lived other people. One could see the trees on their ridges and the flames and smoke of their field-burning; one could often hear the distant drumming from their dances. They might be Lugbara or other peoples, but in the context of social distance this was not relevant. Social ties crossed ethnic boundaries. What was relevant was that they were beyond the limit of everyday social relations. They

[3]Unlike many East African peoples, the Lugbara had no age-classes that could provide a measure of passing time.

were given certain attributes, of which the most common was the possession of magical powers and medicines. Although the limit of everyday relations could not always be measured, it was usually about ten or fifteen miles away across the open plateau, and the magical beings stretched away to the horizon. If someone had actually visited that far, then the particular people visited were regarded as exceptions that proved the rule. I might see the contradiction in a situation in which groups within distant view of each other would describe each other as being magicians and sorcerers, people with evil medicines and the power to turn into stones and trees on the path when one meets them; but for Lugbara the occasion to see the contradiction did not often arise.

Every household thus saw itself as surrounded first by people like themselves, then by a circle of people whose territories were filled with sorcery and magic and who were evilly disposed toward them, even though it was assumed they were Lugbara. But this was relative: when compared to groups beyond them, who were even worse, the closer strangers appeared almost like one's own kin. They were people beyond the bounds of society altogether, and people said of them, "How do we know where they come from, of what deeds they do? We fear them and we do not know them." The most distant of these creatures, beyond the magicians and the sorcerers, were thought to be hardly human in appearance. Although they were never visited, it was maintained that they walked on their heads. Such were the Logo, the Mundu, the 'Bale, and people beyond them, the areas from which the Belgian troops had come. These people ate meat that was rotten, and "bad" meat such as snakes, frogs, hyenas, and other night animals. Peoples such as the Makaraka, the Momvu, the Mangbetu, and the people whom Lugbara knew as Niam-niam, the Azande, were all reputed to be cannibals. They walked upside-

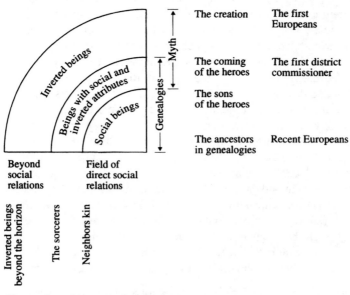

*Categories of time and space.*

down, begot children by their sisters, had terrible types of sorcery, and lived in the thick forests in ways that Lugbara could not understand.

These were not mere fairy stories told for amusement, although they aroused both mirth and horror. Lugbara applied one set of concepts, which others may express only in the separate categories of time and space, both to the mythical and genealogical past and to the contemporary social environment. In mythical and genealogical distance any actual or comparative time scale was irrelevant. All myths had the same thematic pattern. Similarly, any actual or comparative scale of territorial distance was irrelevant to the spatial categories. The same thematic pattern was found whatever the actual physical distance might be. In both schemes the essential distinction was between the near people, members of one's own community and neighborhood, and the distant inverted people, who were beyond social relations and outside genealogical tradition. Each community had its own genealogy, known only to itself, but the same corpus of myth was held by all Lugbara. The limits of social relations that were important for any group were defined by mythical inversion.

There were, of course, degrees of inversion, corresponding to degrees of social distance. In general, inverted beings were asocial and their behavior amoral, but degrees of asociability and amorality varied. The incestuous cannibals were more inverted than the sorcerers, and were socially more remote, being in fact beyond contact altogether. The more remote the being, the more its behavior was conceived as being the utter negation of that to do with kinship: for an ordinary man to ensorcell someone was at least comprehensible, whereas to eat his own children was not.

# 3 / Family, Clan, and Lineage

## THE FAMILY CLUSTER AND ITS ELDER

The smallest domestic unit during my stay and within the memories of the oldest people living at the time was the "hut" *(jo)* occupied by a single wife and her small children. The "compound" *(aku)* was the home of a married man, whether he had one or several wives. Elementary and compound families were grouped into larger residential units that I call family clusters. Each of these had a head, known as *'ba wara* or *'ba ambo* (literally, "big man"), which I translate as "elder."

The family cluster was a small group, generally of about twenty-five people (about six adult men and their wives and children). It was not always a compact unit, though it might be (and probably was in the past). It usually consisted of a scattered group of homesteads, which could be up to half a mile across. The cluster had its own stretch of land, in which were its compounds, fields and grazing, and its own livestock; and its members had a strong sense of "belonging." When the cluster became too large to act as a single family group it might be split in two. Thus at any particular time the unit under the authority of an elder might be a single compound family or a cluster of several families. But whatever its size, it had a single elder and played the same part within a wider system of similar groups. It was the basic unit of Lugbara society. When a man spoke of "home" *(akua,* literally "at the compound") he referred to the family cluster. When a wife visited her parents and natal kin, she visited all the members of the family cluster into which she had been born. Its compounds were "the homes of the ancestors," who were thought to dwell in the earth beneath them. Things fall apart

Lugbara thought of the family cluster as being based upon a small lineage. A lineage consists of people descended in one line from a single founding ancestor. Descent may be through men only (patrilineal) or through women only (matrilineal). The Lugbara lineage was patrilineal. A family cluster typically consisted of adult men who were members of a single lineage, with their wives (who by the rule of exogamy belonged to other lineages), and unmarried children. It is in this sense that I speak of the lineage forming the "core" of a family cluster. There were both small and large lineages. The family cluster was formed around the smallest, which I call a minimal lineage. The lineage was conceived as permanent, persisting over many generations; the family cluster was not. Land and livestock were vested in the lineage, but rights in them were enjoyed by its living members.

The family cluster was controlled and represented by its head, the elder. Like most Lugbara institutions, the office of elder could not be very clearly or precisely defined. His status and authority shaded into those of the heads of junior families,

31

*Two co-wives carrying their babies in leather carrying thongs.*

and these might also be called elders if they were old. But Lugbara always knew whether a man was a "real" elder or not, and the term was properly applied only to those men who by virtue of genealogical position in the lineage held the custodianship of certain shrines. All heads of domestic families whose fathers were dead had shrines to the ghosts of the recent ancestors and various spirits. But an elder, besides having the ordinary ghost shrines of his own homestead, also had special shrines for the ghosts of the founding ancestors of the major lineage and the clan. I call these external lineage shrines. They were built outside the homesteads in a patch of bush, well away from the ghost shrines in the compounds. The elder's spiritual power was associated especially with those shrines that were outside the homesteads and in the bush. This was not a friendly place but was fearsome and even evil. Most men kept away from these external shrines, and only elders ventured there.

An elder had certain traditional insignia of office, although many no longer actually possessed them. The most important was the *ogua,* a special round stool made from a single piece of wood. No one but elders might sit on these stools, and they were inherited. There were other marks of office found in different parts of the country, certain sticks or wands being the most common.

Lugbara defined an elder by saying "a man is called the elder because he eats the chest of meat," or "because he eats the tongue," "because he sits on the *ogua* stool," "because he stays with shrines" (this was partly a reference to his role in war when he stayed behind making offerings to the ghosts during the fighting)," "because he cuts meat at the shrines," "because he puts his hand into the shrines." In parts of northern Lugbara he was called *ori'ba,* which in that area meant "ghost-shrine man." The elder made the actual offerings at most sacrifices and said the ritual

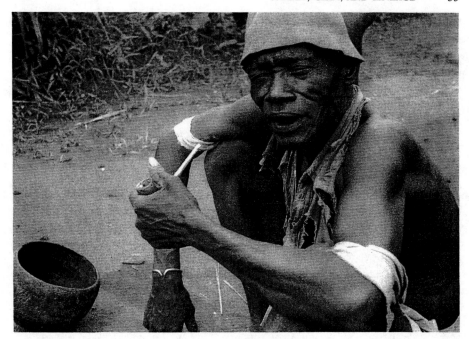

*A respected elder.*

address, and he directed the division of the sacrificial meat. At the distribution certain parts fell to him, to be eaten by him and his chief wife alone. These parts were the spare meat of the chest, the liver, kidneys, testicles, penis, intestines, and usually the tongue. I was told by an elder that "our work is the work of the home," that is, to do with the ghost shrines and the maintenance of peace and good order in the family.

The elder was the senior living descendant of the minimal lineage's ancestors; he was nearest to the most recent of them and was expected to be the first to die and join them. He was a representative of the living members of his lineage to the dead, a role expressed in his powers of cutting and distributing meat. He was also the representative of the dead to their living kin. Thus he had two roles that overlapped to some degree. He was the ritual representative of the lineage and also the head of the family cluster. In the latter role he held religious sanctions over a range of dependents who included people who were not members of his own lineage.

The elder was properly the eldest son of the senior, or first, wife of his predecessor. If a married man inherited a widow from his father, then that wife, if she were married first, became his senior wife and took precedence over the wife whom he had already. "You fear that wife of your father because she is like your mother." She would not, of course, be a man's own mother, but one of his mother's co-wives. In such a case, the heir was the first-born son of that senior wife, even if that son were younger than a son of the junior wife, who had been in fact first married to this particular husband. This principle permitted succession by both son and brother, and led to much wrangling and uncertainty as to succession and inheritance.

This rule of succession referred essentially to the mystical power of being able to sacrifice at the shrines as the nearest direct descendant of the dead ancestors. But in fact the elder so appointed might not be regarded as the elder in all situations. If he were young, weak, or poor, he might be replaced in some situations by a close kinsman who was senior, strong-willed, or wealthy, who would act as a kind of regent in everyday matters.

## THE COMPOSITION OF THE FAMILY CLUSTER

The members of a family cluster consisted of three kinds of people. First there were the members of the minimal lineage, which provided both its name and its elder. This lineage was usually of three to five generations in depth, with up to three generations of living members, who were the descendants of the lineage founder who was thought to have lived a generation or two earlier than the oldest living man. The lineage included both men and women, and daughters married elsewhere remained members of it during their lifetime and after their deaths; however, as in most patrilineal systems, the memory of their names faded after a few generations. In all family clusters some men born into them moved away to settle elsewhere, temporarily or permanently, but they remained lineage members, as did their patrilineal descendants. They, too, might be forgotten in later years if they lived far away and if ties were not maintained by visiting.

A man was expected to respect his senior kin, both living and dead, a child its parents, a wife her husband, a sister her brother, and a younger sibling an older one. Lugbara see "respect" (ru) as obedience, fear, and affection. It is ambivalent, as they realize very well. A man should love his father, who brought him up, protected him, and taught him to become a responsible adult; but at the same time Lugbara observed cynically that a man might "hate his father in his heart," because as long as his father were alive he would be merely a "youth" and economically dependent. "A man loves his father but he waits for him to die." A father should discipline his sons, yet he would not wish to harm them. He might beat his children when they were small, but once they reached adolescence he used religious sanctions against them for all but trivial offenses. It was said that a man would be unwilling to strike his sons with his hand and so he would ask the ghosts to do it for him. He acted in many situations as the representative of the dead members of the lineage, who looked after the well-being and happiness of their living kin. To the living "our ancestors" were near and vivid, for they were the sources of morality and the focus of lineage identity vis-à-vis other lineages.

The relationship between brothers was expected to be one of affection and mutual help between equals. The same term was used for both elder and younger brothers. To call a friend a "brother" was a compliment, and Lugbara often said that important men who were equal in status, such as rainmakers and chiefs, were "like brothers"; in this phrase there was also the connotation that the "brothers" would stand together against outsiders. But Lugbara maintained that most brothers were sometimes jealous of one another over family property, and senior men competed with their brothers for the ritual status of eldership of the family cluster. In such a

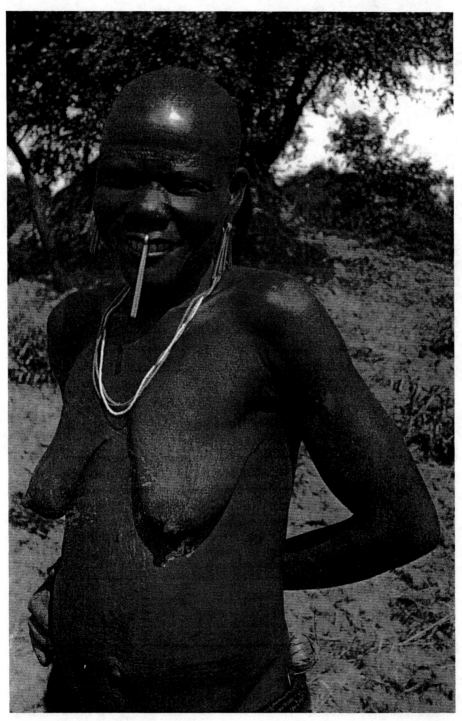

*A woman, aged about fifty when the picture was taken. She wears ear- and lip-rings made locally of iron.*

case the competition might be fought out quite unscrupulously. A man was expected to protect his sister and give her good advice, and sisters to help their brothers when asked. They helped one another particularly in their love affairs, and kept these secret from their parents.

The family cluster also included the wives of lineage members. The head of a family had domestic authority over his wives and children. A wife did not change her lineage at marriage but remained a member of it and under the care of its ancestors all her life. Sacrifices on her behalf were generally made by her father or brothers to their ancestral ghosts, but it was thought that she could also be made sick by the ghosts of her husband's lineage, and in that case her husband's people sacrificed for her. She remained predominantly under her own ancestors' care, and when those of her husband affected her they did so because she was a mother of their descendants rather than because she was a wife. Her position was thus ambivalent: although she never relinquished her affiliation to her natal lineage and its ghosts, in everyday affairs she was under the authority of the senior men of her husband's group, and her natal family and her own ancestors did not intrude so long as she was well treated.

Lastly, a family cluster might include one or two men of different lineages. They were usually the sons or husbands of women who had been born into the lineage. For various reasons they prefered to live with their mothers' or wives' kin. They accepted the authority of their host elder, but their position, like that of wives, was ambivalent, as they still had close ties with their own natal lineage. There might also be clients, unrelated men who attached themselves to rich men as followers and who might be given their daughters as wives.

## NOTIONS OF DESCENT

Lugbara saw their society as being descended from the heroes and their sons through long patrilineal descent lines. These lines consisted of ancestors who were points of articulation between lineages. They varied in depth from eight to thirteen generations.

All Lugbara descent lines went back to a common set of brother-ancestors, the sons of the heroes. Lugbara thought of their tribal unity as being due to ties of "blood" (ari). They said they were "one people" and "all one blood," and so different from Kakwa, Alur, Europeans, and others. This blood came from the Creator Spirit. They used the same expression when speaking of the unity of members of a clan, the group consisting of the patrilineal descendants of a son of one of the heroes. It was generally not used in reference to lineages; of these it was said "people have different bodies, one blood."

Descent was seen as running through both men and women. Patrilineal descent in the direct line could be reckoned for everyone back to the first men placed on earth by Spirit, through one of the heroes and down a direct line of ancestors to living men and women. Descent through women was reckoned for only a few generations, until kin so related were "far away" and forgotten. As far as personal kinship ties were concerned, Lugbara saw little difference in descent through a man or a woman. If a man were killed, his mother ran back to her own people, who came to join in the fighting to avenge his death. I was told by an elder:

> because his blood came from here, from his mother's brother's people. Now her son has died and left only little children. Truly he is our man. If our daughter had been born a man she would have begotten children here with us, but she bore that child there with her husband. Truly he is our child.

Associated with these notions of descent were those of unisexual characteristics. Lugbara said that a man took after his father and a woman after her mother. This was axiomatic, despite what were to me clear exceptions. Physically it was often true. This notion was not often socially significant with regard to men—witchcraft powers, for example, were not in theory inherited, although a witch's son who behaved like his father in other ways might be thought to be one—but in the case of women was connected with their possession by Spirit. This possession gave an adolescent girl the power of divination, which was inherited by daughters. The society was predominantly patrilineal in bias. Descent through a woman might be significant in lineage affiliation for men, but was not so for women: one female link might be accepted as though it were a male link, but more than one were too weak to be significant in lineage matters. There remained the mother-daughter line, which was important neither in inheritance of status or property nor in ritual. It was significant only in the context of divination, which although a socially useful activity was nonetheless associated with evil and was feared.

## CLAN DISPERSAL

Lugbara saw their society as being made up of clans that had spread out and dispersed from the original clan homes where their founders were begotten by the heroes. Once I was talking about this with an old man when we had gone to watch ants moving across a path. It was the beginning of the rains, so streams of ants were everywhere. He said:

> You have heard the words I have said to you. We people are like these ants. Once our ancestors lived separately. Then they wandered among themselves, they wandered across the land like these ants, and now we live together in our little groups. We have come far from the home of our ancestors.

We need not accept clan traditions as relating historically true events, but they were not necessarily untrue in every detail. Most genealogies that told of past relationships with other groups elsewhere probably reflected actual historical events, although there was no way of telling how far back in time they took place. At least we may accept the general theory of dispersal of groups as told by Lugbara. Besides telling of historical events, genealogies were also used to validate groups' present distribution that was in a constant state of change and realignment.

There were in the 1950s at least sixty clans, and it is probable that this is still so today: changes at this level take place extremely slowly. Their founders were the sons of the heroes. These sons had sons in turn, and their patrilineal descendants form the clans that Lugbara regarded as the basic units of their society. They were basic because they were regarded as permanent and above change, although this was not in fact always true. No clan was senior to any other. The order of birth of their founders was unknown, and although they varied in size it was never said that a clan was more important than another merely because it was larger. Each clan had a clan-name, which, like all Lugbara names, had an original meaning that could usually be explained.[1] I use the term "clan-name" to refer also to names given to lineages—many lineages had the same names as clans.

The members of a clan were dispersed and found in many parts of the country. Since the founding of Lugbara society, the descendants of the clan founders, who were the sons of the hero-ancestors, had moved about the country, groups of kin segmenting and moving apart. But there was almost always a main part of a clan that had not split up and that still inhabited a territory associated with the clan. It formed what might be called the localized core of that clan, and I call it a subclan. The founder of a subclan was thus the same man as the founder of the clan. A clan was a shadowy group that consisted of a subclan living in the clan territory and a number of offshoots that had moved away at various times in the past and lived in other clan territories elsewhere. The subclan was the important unit in everyday matters. In the territory associated with it, and that was given its name, lived members of other clans whose ancestors had settled there or who had settled there recently themselves. The total group thus formed what I call a subtribe, which was also given the name of the subclan. I describe the subtribe later in this chapter. Subclans were segmented into smaller descent groups, which I call lineages. The number of generations given in any genealogy from living people to the clan founders was usually from eight to thirteen. It would be possible to trace the supposed genealogical relationships of any two members of a clan or subclan (and therefore of any two Lugbara anywhere) but this was never done.

Proliferation of clans and lineages took place in two ways, as could be observed if not by the anthropologist at least by Lugbara themselves in the course of a lifetime. These were by the expansion and segmentation of a lineage, and by dispersal of individuals who left their parental homes and settled elsewhere, founding lineages of their own. These individuals might be accompanied by their domestic families. Proliferation was usually caused by an increase in numbers and was associated with a migratory drift across the countryside in search of more land. The northern and central parts of Lugbaraland had been longer settled than the south, and most movement has been from the densely occupied north to the emptier south.

Most Lugbara were farmers, so people moved into areas where there was spare land. With the rotation of crops, families were always moving their farms from exhausted to fresh land, so they moved huts and fields every few years into nearby areas where there was either more fresh land or least opposition. Where the land was uniformly occupied, a group moved into the territory of their most distantly related neighbors. All groups resented intrusion. One could not clear land and move

---

[1]Examples were Lariba, "the fig-tree people"; Anyavu, "the eaters"; Anyatibionziku, "we do not eat bad vegetables." Most referred to some characteristic of an ancestor in myth or genealogy, although some were place names only.

into the land of one's close agnates since the elders and (it was believed) the ancestors would object. But to move into the area of an unrelated or less closely related neighbor was less opposed by kinship sanctions, and one's immediate kin would give support in any consequent fighting. In addition, men often moved away and settled with their mothers' or wives' kin as soon as they were married and needed land of their own.

By the 1950s it had become increasingly difficult for groups to move into their neighbors' lands, since the government tried to prohibit movement of this sort. The result had been that more men hived off from their home settlements, taking up land either with a maternal or affinal kinsman or in the peripheral areas of the country. As I have said above, many of these were in fact outside Lugbaraland altogether, in the richer lands of Bunyoro and Buganda.

The general process of migration drift took place both by lineage movement, amoebalike, in one general direction, and by the settlement of individuals and their families elsewhere, usually in the less-populated areas to the south. The routes taken during the slow migration of a group across the countryside were told in legend, in which ancestors were said to have lived in certain places—like the heroic myths, migrations distant in time were expressed in narratives of individual travels—and could be seen in the distribution of burial trees. Every important man and woman had a barkcloth tree planted at the head of his or her grave. The grave itself was covered by stones that were left undisturbed for several years. The tree was never cut, nor its wood or leaves used, and the land immediately surrounding it was not cultivated. It was given the personal name of the individual whose grave it marked. These great trees, often several generations old, were a marked feature of the Lugbara landscape, usually standing alone, although in some areas they formed part of raingroves and so were not noticeable. The burial tree of Dribidu was said still to be visible on Mount Eti. The burial trees of a group's more distant ancestors were usually well outside its present territory, especially in southern Lugbara. In the north they were often still inside the territory, because there had been less recent migration movement there. The migration routes of lineages could be traced across country by the trees of their ancestors. In some cases, of course, as in that of Dribidu, a burial tree was named to be consistent with and thereby confirm belief in a myth or legend.

This process of migration drift had resulted in the dispersal of clans over the countryside. Tradition may not be historically correct in every detail, since details have to fit in with the axiomatic origin of clans near Mounts Eti and Liru; otherwise the process described in tradition might have been observed occurring in the 1950s as it has presumably occurred in the past.


## HOST, ACCESSORY, AND REMNANT GROUPS

I have mentioned that local land shortage might lead people to leave their parental homes and attach themselves to uterine kin, at whose homes they were given land and took up residence. This led in time to the formation of what I call accessory groups attached to host groups. I prefer the term "host" to terms such as "dominant" or "authentic." In Lugbara they were dominant neither politically nor ritually, except that they gave their name to the territory in which they lived. "Authentic" implies that accessory groups are not authentic but may claim to be so, which was not true in this case. I never heard the origin of an accessory group deliberately concealed, but it is possible that in the past this was so, especially when such a group's founding ancestor was in a servile position to the host group, as was a client, usually a poor man without land who attached himself to a wealthy but unrelated man. Inferior origin was sometimes used as a taunt in personal quarrels, but then so was size of a clan that had so dwindled in numbers that it could no longer maintain its own rights, and such groups might be among the oldest and most "authentic" of all. Taunts of this kind reflected numerical weakness rather than inferior origin.

The term for a host group was *kari'ba,* meaning the direct patrilineal descendants of the subclan founder. The terms for accessory groups were variants of words for "stranger"; among High Lugbara I have heard them referred to as "our Madi," that is, as Low Lugbara or strangers.

Accessory groups were usually the descendants of a man who had attached himself to a member of the host group, as a uterine or affinal kinsman or as a client. The original host-client relationship was between individuals and was inherited by their descendants. If the tie were one of mother's brother-sister's son then the accessory group remained as "sisters' sons"; if it were one of brothers-in-law, then it remained so, notwithstanding the fact that this tie became one of mother's brother-sister's son after one generation; and if it were a tie of clientship then it remained so for several generations, although later this might change to a tie of "brothers."

Groups as well as individuals might move and become attached as accessory groups because of famine, warfare, pestilence, or governmental action. Many such groups were scattered along the Uganda side of the Uganda-Congo border because many people moved to flee from the harsh politics of the former Congo administration. This was a modern development, because until European administration had prevented large-scale fighting such a group could not have settled in this way. The hostility and the bitterness that accompanied it were indicative of the values involved in the settlement of accessory groups: a group came only when there were existing kinship ties, not trying to take land belonging to others without entering into the full complex of kinship and neighborly behavior that was part of such a relationship. Those groups that had entered from the Congo were usually in fact allowed to remain, but people said of them, "They are new people; later we shall eat with them." In time, individuals would intermarry, and later the immigrants would be assimilated and become accessory lineages proper of the groups on whose boundaries they lived.

The system could absorb attached individuals, who might become the founders of later accessory groups, but it could not easily absorb immigrant groups, with the one exception of the Ndu smiths, who were found throughout Lugbaraland; but these formed an exception that did not disprove the generalization, inasmuch as they came as smiths and not as farmers. It is significant that their position was one surrounded by mystical sanctions of many kinds. The absorption of individuals meant that they had to be enmeshed in a network of kinship and neighborhood ties in order to lead any kind of social life. Even if they were culturally different—as Kakwa who attached themselves to Lugbara hosts—they became Lugbara in culture as soon as they took up residence with their hosts. This type of attachment was very much like that of Dinka in Nuer lineages, and of quite a different order from that of heterogeneous groups among neighboring peoples such as the Madi and Alur. Among both these peoples alien groups were absorbed partly by means of the institution of chiefship, which supplied a symbol of unity to groups of diverse origin, and which was lacking in Lugbara. Also, the nature of the linking of component lineages within the subtribe was different, the Lugbara being very like the Nuer in this respect, but very different from the Madi and Alur (Middleton and Tait 1958; Evans-Pritchard 1940; Southall 1956).

Besides creating new ties between themselves and their host groups, the dispersal of attached groups and individuals widened the network of kinship ties of which their parent group was the center. An attached person maintained close ties with his parent lineage, since he was dependent upon its members ritually and in certain other ways, of which the most important was that his host would not make himself responsible for supplying the settler with bridewealth, most of which had to come from his father. If he stayed and founded a lineage these patrilineal ties became less and less recognized until after a generation or two they were forgotten.

Any genealogical account of a clan or lineage mentioned movement of ancestors in the distant and semimythical past. Reference was made to the origin of groups that had moved elsewhere and were never visited. A group twenty or thirty miles away was usually beyond visiting range, although visible across the open plateau. These traditions made sense of and gave a pattern to the expanse of densely occupied country that was visible from any of the rocky outcrops that were scattered over the countryside and on which men took the air, women dried grain and clothes, and children played.

A lineage was named by the clan-name of the ancestors three or four generations back, by whom it was differentiated from other lineages. If, for example, the founder of the lineage that was segmenting had two wives, the lineage would split into two, and each new segment would take as its new clan-name that of the wife from whom its members were directly descended. They thus recognized distant kin ties with the group from which that wife had come before her marriage. Lineages bearing the same clan-name were thus linked either because they belonged to the same clan, or because they were the "sisters' sons" of the group from which they had taken their name. These distant ties of clanship composed a network covering all Lugbara society and extended into neighboring societies. This was often the object of comment by my Lugbara companions. I was struck by the degree of hospitality, exemplified by the giving of food, beer, and labor to prepare the food, extended to us when we visted a group with which someone could establish kinship of this shadowy type. Also, proper kinship terms were used. This was especially noticeable on the one or two occasions when the ties were those of patrilineal clanship, but sometimes we found ourselves among "mothers' brothers" of a range so distant as to be impossible to reckon; but it was said it must exist and efforts were always made to find the tie by genealogical reckoning.

Clans sometimes dwindle in size and die out. Members of a descent group that had decreased in numbers would say "now we have all died, there are no people, we eat food by ourselves." The metaphor was that of ritual eating of food together, one of the basic norms of kinship. There were no related groups left to share sacrificial meat. Members of these groups said that they feared above all the destruction of their shrines, in which they placed offerings for their ancestral ghosts, after the group had ceased to exist among the living. If this happened no one would place food for them in their turn and even the idea of the lineage might be extinguished. The shrines were taken by the lineage most closely related and placed in the grass away from the homesteads. The head of the caretaker lineage made offerings as long as the livestock of the group that had died out remained. When the last member of the group died it was soon forgotten, even to its burial trees, which were the sole remaining signs of its existence.

There were many such groups that had dwindled to a few members. They were called "clans which remain," and I call them remnant clans. They consisted of members who might be scattered over what had once been their own territory but had become so reduced in numbers that the territory had been occupied by encroaching groups from other areas. Some of these remnant clans were still fairly large, with a few dozen members, but others had only two or three old men waiting to die. There might be no sons and the daughters might have married elsewhere, or perhaps the sons had moved away to live with mothers' brothers because there was no longer any land or livestock for them to inherit. Such groups were found everywhere. They still had their own heads, but could never act as independent political units. Although so few in numbers, they still had full-length clan genealogies stretching back to the heroes. They were not important enough for other groups to know anything about their genealogies, but their own heads related them at great length and pointed with pride to their burial trees as proof of their past.

## THE LINEAGE SYSTEM

The inner workings of the subtribe and the subclan need some explanation. The Lugbara had what is called a segmentary lineage system. This meant that they were organized into small groups that were regarded as being segments of larger groups. As segments they were distinct and their members thought of themselves as forming separate groups in certain situations; but in other situations they joined together to form larger units. These larger units might in their turn join with other similar units to form still larger ones. At each level the units were thought of as equivalent. The total system was regarded as constant, but the component groups were always changing; smaller groups might grow large and then segment to form two or more segments.

Lugbara conceived almost all social relations—certainly long-lasting ones—as operating within the framework of this system, and so I could understand little of their social life without a knowledge of it. A difficulty that faced the fieldworker in Lugbara is that they themselves could not—or at least did not—describe this system in abstract terms; they took it for granted. For me to make sense of it, I must use several concepts (lineage, segment, section, and others) for which the Lugbara themselves had no specific terms. In this account I use the terms first used in this sense by Evans-Pritchard in his classic work on the Nuer (Evans-Pritchard 1940; see also Fortes and Evans-Pritchard 1940, and Middleton and Tait 1958).

The reader may well wonder why it is necessary for the anthropologist to use these special terms to describe a society whose members did not themselves find it necessary to do so. Anthropologists are sometimes accused of building up a needlessly complex structural model, while the people they are studying seem to manage very well without it. In the case of a people like the Lugbara the reason is simple, but I think it is important to state it. The Lugbara "lived" their society; they did not have to describe it or analyze it so as to make sense of it to outsiders. For Lugbara, the range of everyday social relations, the context of everyday life was narrow. They were concerned with at the most about a score of small local groups and lineages. They were brought up from childhood to know where they were on the ground and how their founding ancestors were related to one another. They learned exactly how to behave to the members of these groups, and what to expect from them. They referred to them by their clan-names, or merely as "mothers' brothers," "patrilineal kin," and so on. But I was in a different position. I was, in a sense, outside and above the society. I moved from one part of the country to another and soon perceived that the organization of local groups was not haphazard but had a regular pattern. Most Lugbara were unaware of this because they did not travel far; they neither had to learn the internal organization of other groups, nor were they much interested in them. To describe this pattern, which is found throughout Lugbara, I required special terms that were not needed by the people themselves. But they could see the point of these terms when I explained it to them. I found that when I described the overall pattern to individual Lugbara, they saw it immediately, and were both pleased and, sometimes, surprised to learn that their local organization was not unique to themselves but was found among all Lugbara.

Lugbara said that the basic units of their society were the sixty-or-so clans. As I have mentioned, the effective divisions of these clans were the sub-clans. Apart from all Lugbaraland and the vaguely defined groups marked by differences of dialect or material culture, the largest local group was that formed around a subclan. I call this group a subtride, and it consisted of the men born into the subclan who had lived in the subtribe territory and not moved elsewhere, their wives and unmarried children, and various attached groups. Its structure was similar to that of the family cluster but on a larger scale: the family cluster included about twenty-five people, the subtribe about four thousand.

A subtribe usually comprised between 150 and 200 family clusters, although many were smaller and many were larger than this. The family clusters were the largest groups, small as they were, with heads who held internal authority: these were the elders. Family clusters were grouped for certain purposes into larger units, which I call minor sections; minor sections were grouped into still larger ones, which I call major sections; and major sections joined together to form subtribes. There might be more section levels, but these were typical. Most subtribes included from four to eight major sections, each comprising about twenty-five family clusters grouped into from two to four minor sections; each minor section had from two to ten family clusters. Obviously, these figures might vary, but what I have described was a typical subtribe.

Each of these levels of local grouping was concerned with various activities. The subtribe was the largest group within which disputes had ultimately to be settled by agreement. The major section was—or had been in the traditional system—the feuding unit. Within it disputes were settled by discussion or the operation of religious sanctions, because its members were regarded as too closely related by kinship for the exercise of force to be justifiable between them. At the lowest level the family cluster was the basic residential and political group. The minor section could not be very clearly defined. It consisted of several family clusters that had been until recently a single family cluster, and had recently segmented, so that ties of kinship were still extremely close between its members but they no longer recognized the authority of a single elder. This organization may be illustrated by a simple diagram:

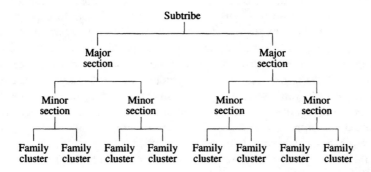

Here I have shown each group as consisting of only two segments of a lower order. In some cases a group had in fact only two segments, but it might have three or four.

I have said that all descendants of the original clan founders had not remained in the original clan territories. Many had become dispersed and had attached themselves to host lineages in various parts of the country. A man might attach himself as sister's son, sister's husband, or as a client, and his descendants then formed an accessory lineage attached to that of his orginal host. The cluster of lineages thus formed was a section. A section did not always contain accessory lineages, but at least it always included its members' wives, who were not members of their husbands' lineages, by the rule of clan exogamy.

A section was a local group composed of people living in families: they were real people living on the ground. But a lineage, as Lugbara conceived it, was a descent group, consisting of both ancestors and their living descendants: one could not see a lineage, although one could see those members of it who were alive. Lineage unity was an important value. Thus women born into a lineage and married elsewhere returned home from time to time, especially on the occasion of sacrifice to their ancestors by the lineage elders. Certain rights were vested in lineages, the principal ones being those in the resources of land, livestock, and men and women. Their living members acted together in certain situations, such as those of marriage, ritual, fighting and feud, and dancing at funerals. Many of the living members of a lineage were likely to be living in different sections, but they were still thought of as composing a corporate group in which certain rights were vested. This group was thought of by Lugbara as permanent, whereas they knew that a section might form and disband in time.

To understand how this system worked I have had to make this distinction between lineage and section. But the Lugbara did not do so in everyday speech. A section was merely given the name of its host lineage. A lineage system therefore reflected the system of sections (see diagram on page 44), and provided for Lugbara the idiom in which the section system was conceived:

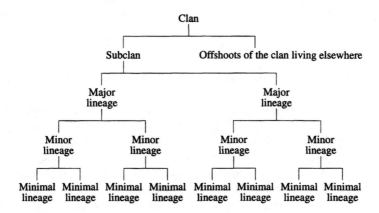

Every lineage, of whatever size, had a founder whose name was remembered by his living descendants. In this way a genealogy preserved the memory of the ancestors and also charted the distribution of the component lineages of any sub-clan. At the same time it indicated the distribution on the ground of the various sections that were associated with these lineages.

This system enabled the Lugbara to think of their society, and particularly of their own subtribe, as having order and stability. In fact, the family clusters that composed the subtribe were always moving about in search of new fields and hut sites. Some might die out, others might increase in number and segment into new family clusters, still others might attach themselves to lineages elsewhere as accessory groups. Lugbara made sense of this fluid situation by thinking of it in terms of lineage and genealogy. Whether or not a man moved from one part of the subtribe territory to another, his status in the lineage and his position in its genealogy remained fixed. Also, the continuity of lineages through time, as corporate groups, was thought of in the same way. Due to demographic, ecological, and other factors, the system of sections was in constant change, but the system of lineages was seen as permanent. By reference to it Lugbara could see their society as coherent and stable.

Lugbara had generic names for these groups, the words *ori'ba* and *suru*. *Ori'ba* meant "ghost people"—*ori* was the ghost of an ancestor for whom a shrine had been built by his descendants—and consisted of a group of people who shared common ghost shrines. *Ori'ba* were primarily those groups under the ritual authority of an elder. They were typically minimal and minor lineages and sections.

*Suru* had the meaning of a group of people who considered themselves and were considered by others to form a group because they shared a territory and had ties between them based on common ancestry. The ritual content of the ties that bound members of an *ori'ba* was absent. Thus *suru* referred to major lineages and sections, clans, subclans, and subtribes. The term was used also in a wider sense as the *suru* (people) of Madi or Europeans, and as "species" or "category," as in a *suru* of birds or trees. This is not to say that Lugbara saw birds and trees as organized into lineages—although since all creatures are descended from those put in Meme's womb by the Creator Spirit there was something of this idea present, and cattle were definitely classed by lines of descent from ancestral cattle whose names were remembered—but as being differentiated from other creatures with different characteristics.

## RAINMAKERS AND HOLDERS OF POLITICAL AUTHORITY

The Lugbara have had neither king nor traditional chiefs. The head of the minimal lineage held domestic authority over all members of his family cluster. Those elders who were also genealogically the heads of minor and major lineages had no domestic authority over any but their own family clusters, but they might act as representatives of the minor or major lineages on ritual occasions. They were still called only elders. They might wield very considerable influence by virtue of their position but they would not be superior in internal authority to genealogically junior elders of the same lineage. A fairly senior man said of one extremely respected elder, the genealogical head of a major lineage: "We fear the words of Olima. He speaks slowly and is never angry or quarrelsome. Truly he is an elder and we little men follow his words. He leads us like a bull leads his herd of cattle." But when I asked whether Olima would intervene in a dispute in a family cluster other than his own, I was told, "He is the elder of that lineage there, and we do not listen to what he says. Here our elder is Draa and we follow him." This elder's influence was considerable enough for the local county chief to ask for his opinions and heed them, but it did not extend to the internal affairs of lineages other than his own minimal lineage.

There have been certain other functionaries who exercised some political authority. Besides the elders there were men called *opi*, the word used in the 1950s also for county chiefs in the system of government-appointed chiefs. *Opi* were strongest in northern Lugbara, presumably because this was the longest settled area and southern Lugbara was largely occupied by small dispersed groups that had moved there from the north; important men and their lineages were less likely to move than poorer men. Information about the *opi* is confused. Their traditional powers had been taken from them, and there was still much bitterness about the way in which some of the lesser ones had been made chiefs by the Belgians, with powers quite beyond anything they originally possessed, while the "true" *opi* were ignored. Members of the lineages of those made chiefs by the Belgians, having inherited the position, exaggerated the traditional powers of the *opi* to make them equal to those of the chiefs under colonial rule. Other government chiefs and those traditional *opi* who had not been given administrative powers denigrated each other and minimized the others' powers. During my stay, for example, there was considerable unrest in one area of northern Lugbara due to the amalgamation of the territories of certain of these functionaries, a consequence of which was that the power of the government chiefs was further increased at the expense of the traditional *opi*, whose existence and affiliations were ignored. There was fighting, and feeling against the administration ran very high. The traditional *opi* were almost in hiding and were gathering support for their traditional powers, while the government chiefs did not dare to go into these areas. During my stay the colonial administration also introduced the practice of having subcounty chiefs elected instead of being appointed by chiefs. The consequence was the heavy defeat of certain candidates who were sons of county chiefs, and commoners were elected in their place.

The various indigenous functionaries called *opi* all held rudimentary political authority. The most important have been the rainmaker chiefs, *opi-ezo*, ("chiefs of rain"). The power to make and control rain was thought to run in certain descent lines and was limited to one such line in a subclan. It was usually, but not always, the genealogically senior descent line. Inheritance of the power was limited to the rainmaker's own minimal lineage, and this was so important that if a rainmaker had no sons but only daughters the power might be inherited through the eldest daughter to her son, who was adopted into her natal lineage for the purpose. Rainmaking power was held by the custodian of certain sacred objects—rainstones, obsidian necklaces, and iron hoes of a peculiar type[2]—handed down from the earliest ancestors who received them from the Creator spirit. Rain was made by the manipulation of the rainstones, which were kept in oil-filled pots hidden in rain groves.

Rainmakers had other roles besides that of controlling rain, although most of them were no longer important. A man who was the victim of a quarrel could go to the rainmaker and clasp his feet. He was then under the protection of the rainmaker, who would summon the elders of the persons concerned and discuss the matter. He could at one time administer poison ordeals and could forbid continuance of the offense. A rainmaker had the power to forbid fighting between lineages of the same subtribe, by the exercise of his curse. He had the power to try suspected witches and persistent evildoers by ordeal, involving the eating of earth from the grave of a man whose death had been caused by the suspect. He could purify men who had killed opponents in fighting. The general respect paid to him was extreme—especially when contrasted to the general lack of overt respect paid by Lugbara to anyone in authority over them, in particular to appointed chiefs—and his person could not be touched in anger without incurring mystical penalties.

There were also *opi* called *'ba rukuza* ("men whose names are known"). They had secular powers rather than ritual ones. They were well-known and wealthy men, who had many clients and followers. They did not transmit the title to their descendants. In the past they had wielded very considerable power and influence and were said to have arbitrated in disputes, as did rainmakers. But they had no formal authority and no religious sanctions for their power. "They are like great

---

[2]Rainstones were either of quartz (*si*, the word used also for hail, both quartz and hail thought of as falling from the sky) or granite, and were "male" and "female." There is no obsidian in Lugbara, and I do not know the source of the necklaces. The hoes were similar to those used by the Bari-speaking groups to the north.

*Maro, the rainmaker of Vura, a highly respected and wise old man.*

trees in the forest, they support and give strength to everyone," it was said of them. They were said to have carried special white spears or staves as marks of rank. At times of famine people would come from great distances to attach themselves to them as clients in return for food and assistance. There had also been temporary war leaders, the status, a very informal one, being dependent on individual prowess and ability.

'*Ba rukuza* were found mainly in northern Lugbara. In that area also were men called *adro'ba* ("spirit-men"), who had the power to utter curses against persistent evildoers. Formerly they walked with a spear and a bundle of arrows, with a special armlet. Both they and the '*ba rukuza* were scattered throughout subtribes and sections irrespective of the distribution of descent groups. On the other hand, there was usually only one rainmaker in each subclan, his status depending upon genealogical position rather than on individual personal qualities.

Rainmakers were ritual functionaries who had certain political and judicial roles associated with their ritual attributes. The *'ba rukuza* and *adro'ba* may have arisen primarily as a response to outside Arab, European, and other ethnic contacts. At least it may be said that these contacts increased their importance. Many of the *'ba rukuza* had influence over very large areas, especially in the north and northeast, the only parts of Lugbara subjected to prolonged Arab contact. As I have said earlier, some of them were made chiefs by the Belgians because they were the only men with any obvious influence extended over wide areas, and later they, their brothers, sons, or sisters' sons were made chiefs under the British. None were rainmakers. They were not found, so far as I know, in southern Lugbara. In general, the relationship between government chiefs and rainmakers was unfriendly. The latter saw the former as upstarts and "Europeans," and I was told that "To say we are big men and brothers, like these county and subcounty chiefs do now, is bad; *opi* do not do that."

# 4 / The Wider Community

## INTERLINEAGE RELATIONS AND LAW AND ORDER

The Lugbara traditionally lacked any form of kingship or even chiefship. They also lacked any codified law. There were, traditionally, neither courts nor machinery for enforcing legal decisions made in the light of codified jural offenses and punishments. It is sometimes said that members of societies such as this depend upon self-help to enable them to right their wrongs and maintain social order. Yet clearly uncontrolled self-help would lead to anarchy. Lugbara told me that the exercise of both authority and power were essential for the orderly operation of their society. The exercise of power alone was a sign of lack of close social relationships, whereas that of authority, which is both legitimate and responsible, distinguished them from both the mythical figures at the beginning of the world and those "inverted" people living beyond the fringes of their world. All legitimate authority was controlled by the ancestors, who originated orderly social life. They controlled relations within the local community, and used mainly religious sanctions to that end. When these broke down between people who did not recognize the same recent ancestors, then self-help became the only means of keeping order, but even so, it was subject to various controls that prevented it from erupting into mere anarchic violence.

Everyday life for Lugbara was concerned with growing crops; attending markets and dances; meeting kin, friends, and neighbors and eating, drinking, and talking with them; and marriage and courtship. Formerly an important activity was fighting; its place had been taken by attendance at and discussion about cases dealt with at the courts of government-appointed chiefs. Most of these activities were shared with one's neighbors, the members of one's local community. I met many old Lugbara who had never been more than ten miles from the compound in which they were born, but I met others with the most amazing history of traveling. Traditionally there was a certain amount of contact over long distances, with trading expeditions, groups attending the death dances of distant kinsmen, and traveling for food in times of periodic famines. Young people would walk many miles to visit their lovers, and most young men went outside Lugbaraland altogether to work in southern Uganda for a period to earn money for taxes and bridewealth. But in general, and for most people, nearly all everyday activities took place within a small neighborhood a few miles across and never very far from one's own homestead—and almost always within sight of it. A woman changed her home at marriage and therefore was a member of two small neighborhoods, but they were usually close enough together to permit regular visiting.

The formalized relations of everyday life—such as those having to do with marriage—were conceived in terms of categories of kin, which I discuss below, but other relations might not be so conceived. People said that they went to trade with "the people of such and such a place." All places in the country were named. The territories of sections and subtribes were named after the lineages and subclans that occupied them as hosts; hills, valleys, outcrops of rock, streams, clumps of trees and single trees, even if not burial trees, all had names. Thus in situations in which lineage ties were not primarily significant these names of places were used to refer to the people concerned. People did not attend markets, for example, as members of lineage groups as such. The women of a kin group might walk to market together, and if selling might set out their goods on the ground together, but this was incidental to the exchange of goods between individuals. Although the situation was permeated by kinship considerations—a woman would give better terms to a kinswoman than to a stranger—lineage ties were not significant in the main activity. Here, and in many other situations, such as the watching of death dances, which always attracted large crowds of neighbors, people tended to stand and talk and drink according to lineage affiliation, but this affiliation was not primarily significant. It was merely that kinsmen, close friends, and neighbors tended to be the same people. Lineage ties were so all-embracing that it was sometimes difficult to distinguish formalized lineage ties from unformalized ties. The distinction lay mainly in the sanctions underlying them, that is, whether or not the ancestors and their ghosts were involved.

Before discussing the nature of relations between lineages and sections of varying span, I mention two important concepts used by Lugbara. I have described the formal structure of sections and lineages in terms of which relations between them were conceived. This is a formal structure, a paradigm by which Lugbara comprehended their society as having consistency and permanence both in space and time. Local groups were small in numbers and in size, and with the high density of population the political relations of a given family cluster covered a considerable number of other groups—agnatically related, related through uterine kinship, ties of clientship, ties of clanship, and so on. The hopeless confusion in which I found myself after a few months of study of Lugbara local groups was inevitable when trying to sort out the composition and interrelationships of these myriad little clusters of people. The pattern of lineages was continually changing, as they changed in size, segmented, or merged with others. The names of the lineages with which people come into contact were never likely to be the same for very long. Lugbara, like anyone else, seemed to need to imagine their society as stable, and ignored the continual changing in the pattern of groups around them on the ground. They could do this by the use of certain categories that referred to social distance.

At the center of a man's social life was his homestead, and beyond that the homesteads of his family cluster. Beyond that lay the homesteads of his *o'dipi* and *juru*. I cannot find suitable English translations for these terms, and shall have to ask the reader to accept the Lugbara words. *O'dipi* comprised those groups that were related patrilineally, but including also others near them, such as sisters' sons living in the same family cluster. The range of *o'dipi* and their composition varied in different situations, sometimes being close patrilineal kin only, sometimes close patrilineal kin and attached uterine kin, and sometimes including more distant patrilineal kin. Beyond the range of *o'dipi* were the *juru*. *Juru* and *o'dipi* together comprised all those groups with which a person, as a member of a family cluster, had direct social relations, although the further limits of *juru* were not very clearly demarcated. *Juru* did not stretch away to the ends of the earth, but were people who, though unrelated by kinship or whose kin relationship was irrelevant on a given occasion, were nevertheless in a social relationship. In the context of fighting, one fought with arrows against *juru* and not against *o'dipi;* in that of exogamy, one married *juru* and not *o'dipi*. In these two cases the range of *o'dipi* varied; one might fight people whom one could not marry because they were too closely related. Territorially some *juru* would be closer than some *o'dipi,* but socially they were more distant. They were conceptual categories and not groups, although, of course, they had reference to groups.

*Juru* thus extended to the limits of social relations. At the limit of *juru* were those groups with which there were indirect social relations, such as distant kin of people with whom one was in a state of feud. It may be said, more or less, that the limits of a group's *juru* coincided with the range of sorcerers and magicians, in the scheme of sociospatial categories mentioned in Chapter 2, but Lugbara did not usually put the two sets of concepts into a single scheme of thought. They avoided inconsistency and contradiction by using terms applied according to situation rather than to span or genealogical depth.

*Juru* were essentially groups between which any religious sanction was lacking. In actual situations involving the threat of force—the only sanction if religious sanctions were not operative—it was actual sections and lineages that were concerned. The relationship of *juru* had to be translated, as it were, into that between local groups as they were on the ground. The subjectively defined and relative *juru* were composed of objectively defined sections and lineages. The former were units in the conceptual scheme, the latter units in the actual political system. Political relations were those that were ultimately settled by the use of socially approved force, that is, they were concerned with conflicts of interests between groups that could be settled only by fighting. Within the smaller groups fighting did not occur, because ties of kinship were stronger and religious sanctions became operative. The point at which these kinship ties became too weak to prohibit fighting varied from one subtribe to another. Like every situation in Lugbara, it was relative. Political relations shaded into those that were not political.

## FEUD AND WARFARE

Lugbara society seems always to have been in a constant state of instability, which has arisen from conflict of interests between groups and persons. There have been several ways in which these conflicts could be controlled. One has been by the various institutions that have prevented or at least mitigated open hostility. These have included the recognition of lineage ties between units likely to be in conflict, so that open hostility has become a breach of lineage and kinship ties. Another way has been by blood compensation, so that fighting once started could at least be stopped without prolonging it for vengeance. Still another way of controlling conflicts has been by calling into operation various legal, religious, and other sanctions.

It is an old anthropological hypothesis that the significance of an offense is defined not only by its intrinsic nature, nor by its motive, but by the social distance between the parties concerned. This held good for the Lugbara. Here I am referring to the traditional system. Since the coming of the European administration there had developed a new category of offenses that were offenses because of their intrinsic nature, such as tax evasion or refusal to perform such tasks as attending sleeping-sickness inspections, cutting grass for sleeping-sickness clearance, supplying grain, building granaries for famine reserves, and so on. Admittedly, when they were considered before chiefs' courts the relationship of offender to chief might not be entirely irrelevant, but on the whole offenses were judged on their merits, the main aim of the administration in this sphere. Also, chiefs had been appointed who were outside the traditional system of authority altogether, with the power to use force of a type previously unknown. Judgment and the means of enforcing it had little or nothing to do with the status of the offender. On the other hand, traditionally, the status of an offender was strictly relevant to the response against him for the offense, since only certain kinds of force could in fact be brought to bear by the local community. These were violence, various types of mystical sickness believed to be sent in various ways, ostracism, banishment, and occasionally mutilation or severe beating, sometimes to death, by members of the local community. The approval of at least a fair proportion of community members was needed before any of these could be made effective. Lugbara saw most ties between members of a community in terms of kinship, and because one of the most sacred duties of kinship was support for a fellow kinsman or kinswoman, it was not always easy to acquire sufficient support, by an individual or a group, to control an offender.

Except for certain types of violence, these traditional sanctions were still used in the 1950s and traditional offenses that called them into operation still occurred. The system of administration operated by officers of the central government and the district local government (including the chiefs) was found side by side with the traditional organization. Every individual felt the indirect effects of administration, but it was only the heads of families who were directly concerned with its agents, the chiefs and headmen. The remainder of the population spent their lives without ever being directly and personally concerned with the newly imposed system.[1]

Disputes in Lugbara were about the distribution and enjoyment of rights over the resources of land, livestock, and women, and about the maintenance, abuse, or usurpation of status and authority, both of the living and of the dead. They were expected in the history of development of any lineage. It was in the nature of things for lineages to proliferate, segment, amalgamate with others, and even die out. These processes were given meaning and expressed in terms of disputes between their members, just as migrations of clans were told in terms of the wanderings of individual ancestors who quarreled among themselves. Fighting was an important social activity, as the myths of the heroes made plain. Lugbara did not analyze their

[1]There were some exceptions that were becoming more important. One was the need to vote for chiefs and members of political parties, which was only in the first stages during my stay. And the other, of course, was the need for younger men to work as labor migrants for a period.

disputes and their underlying causes any more than we usually do. Like ourselves, they saw them generally as arising from the disagreement of quarrelsome individuals and from the apparent anarchy of everyday life. But a more careful analysis can produce a more meaningful pattern.

Lugbara have never fought wars of conquest. Warfare against Kakwa, Madi, and other neighboring peoples seems to have been due mainly to pressure of population and the need for new land by border groups, and was of the same order as warfare between subtribes within the boundaries of Lugbaraland. Because families on the borders married across them, disputes were often over bridewealth transfers, as among Lugbara themselves, and the fighting seems to have been no more brutal or prolonged than within Lugbaraland.

The most valuable resource in the country has always been land. Every household was dependent upon the use of the various types of land I have mentioned earlier, and any wife who could not get adequate fields complained to her husband. There was constant bickering between wives of a family cluster over the allocation of fields. Allocation was difficult, since provision had to be made for each field type, grazing, and such resources as firewood, trees, water, and even granite outcrops for drying grain and cassava. A woman whose compound was farther from water or rocky outcrops than those of other wives complained that if her fields had been only better sited she would have had an easier time and could have worked better in her fields. Demands for land, wealth, respect, and so on, all led to the building up of tensions. How these were expressed and which set of demands was given precedence depended on factors such as the richness or poverty of soil or grazing, the abundance or scarcity of water, reeds, clay, and so on, and also on personality. Lugbara recognized that some people were better-tempered than others, that some were greedy, some aggressive, others gentle, and others lazy.

Land became scarce through increase in population and decrease in soil fertility, the former being the more important. In the past, lineages would fight against one another for land, beginning with skirmishing between individuals as a consequence of trespass, such as the grazing or clearing of another group's fallow fields. The other most common reason for fighting between groups was that of a wife who ran away from her husband. Her group usually refused to return the bridewealth or returned only a portion of it. Then either the husband's group captured one of her lineage as a hostage to be killed if the bridewealth were not repaid, or the husband took some of her family livestock in reparation. Other common reasons were the seduction of a girl followed by refusal to pay the seduction fine, adultery, drunken quarrels and assault, accusations of witchcraft, and quarrels arising from oracular sessions and the theft of livestock without cause. Lugbara men said that women are "evil," causing strife and trouble to everyone who comes into contact with them. The high proportion of disputes over women was shown by the proportion of cases brought to chiefs' courts. Because fighting was now prohibited, cases that in the past would have led to fighting came to the chiefs, and most cases in courts involved women. Other cases were still settled in traditional ways not involving fighting. Disputes resulting in cases being taken to chiefs' courts were more prevalent among groups living at a high density and suffering from considerable land shortage. It also depended largely upon the personality of the local chief or subchief whether people took cases to him at all; some disputes that would once have been settled by fighting might not come to a chief in one area but would be taken to court in another.

Lugbara men talked about fighting nostalgically and at length, as an example of the ideal life in the happy days now gone as a consequence of the "words of the Europeans." Fighting was forbidden by the administration. It still broke out but was quickly stopped by the chiefs and rarely spread to other than the immediate families of the individuals involved. But all men over middle age and many younger men had taken part in proper fighting—up to the late 1920s—and their information would seem to have been reliable, although perhaps prone to excited exaggeration when describing fighting in which the speaker's own lineage had been involved.

The weapons used by Lugbara were arrows, spears, and clubs. The arrows were headed and barbed, and often smeared with the poisonous juice of the euphoria tree. They could be shot accurately up to about thirty yards. Spears were about four feet long, with blades about a foot long. They could be thrown but were usually used in close combat and could give serious wounds. Clubs were of many kinds, all being of wood and often studded with pieces of metal. Most Lugbara fighting was between small groups of men who would creep up to their enemy and shoot off a volley of arrows. Once the element of surprise was lost they would stand in lines and shoot more arrows, then close in for spear fighting. Although old men gave the impression that fights lasted days and even weeks and involved whole major sections and even subtribes, it is clear that they were sporadic, and were the immediate concern of only a few men at any one time. Killing and even serious wounding were not all that common. The shouting of abuse was often as important a way of letting off steam as actual wounding and killing.

A group would not fight with arrows and spears against members of the same minor lineage, or in some cases of the same major lineage, the group called *ori'ba.* Its being called *ori'ba* ("ghost people") showed that within it relations were sanctioned by the ghosts and by mystical powers rather than by open force exercised by living members. Quarrels within this group were with fists and sticks only. They arose for personal reasons and were stopped by the elders or by onlookers. When women fought, by striking their combatants' mouths with the sides of their hands and by pulling their hair, kicking, and biting, it was the duty of their husbands and brothers to stop them. These fights were always individual and personal, and were quite different from intergroup fighting with weapons, which was traditionally the activity of men.

A group fought with weapons against other groups that it called *juru,* those outside the major section. *Juru* did not mean "enemy" but referred to those groups that might be fought with weapons. When the groups actually fought, they became *ari'ba* ("blood men").

A man killed by a member of his own major section, but of a different minor section, was avenged by the killing of any man of his minor section. If the victim were of a more distant relationship to the killer, retaliation would be made on a member of his major section. Retaliation was made at night. "They came upon our people at night 'like a bomb.' How could they know whether they chose to kill a host member of a stranger attached to that lineage?" an informant said to me when relating the history of past feuds of his lineage. He said:

When you walked among *juru* you did not fear. They did not kill you on sight. They said, "Perhaps this man comes to see our sisters and to sleep with them; he does no ill." If your lineage lost a man or woman who had gone to visit another lineage, if he did not return, you went to look for him. Then slowly you heard they had killed him. Then at night you went to kill those people; men of our lineage without counting went there to kill as many as they could. They came back, having killed many, perhaps five, perhaps ten. They came here to fight, the enemies closed their hearts to die. The elder consulted his rat oracle, perhaps his chicken oracle, to see whether they would be successful. Now it was fighting (*adi*) and it did not stop. People entered secretly to kill. Then the elders tired of these things and slowly they went to mend words among themselves.

Such fighting might last a week or a month, but apparently rarely longer, although it might break out again on a later occasion without much provocation. There were no set times in the year for fighting: "Could you choose when people come to kill you?" I was asked. But it was unlikely for fighting to continue during the times of clearing fields, planting, or harvesting.

Most intergroup fighting was over women. Therefore it was relatively uncommon among patrilineally related lineages between which marriage was forbidden. *Juru* in this context included groups related to a minimal lineage, as one of its member's wife's kin, since it was usually among affines that fighting over women started. The distinction was clear between intergroup and interpersonal ties. In fighting as a member of his lineage against a lineage in which he, as an individual, had ties of maternal or affinal kinship, a man would try not to shoot arrows at his own kinsmen. He would shout at them to stand aside but if they did not do so loyalty to his own lineage would prevail and he might shoot them. I know of a few men who found themselves in this position. They had to go to their dead kinsman's home to mourn his death. There such a visitor could not be killed since the killers would have died "of his blood," but they might try to kill him for vengeance on the way back once they had left their territory or later if they avenged the death. Also such a man was liable to receive a much feared curse from his mother, who would take off her pubic leaves and throw them at her son, saying: "I bore you and now you kill my brother." As a lineage member a man had to fight on the side of his "brothers," but tried not to harm his own maternal or affinal kinsman; however, his half-brothers might kill his mother's kin, and "brothers" by different fathers might kill his affines, since they did not themselves have the same ties.

Fighting among groups of the same subtribe could be stopped by the joint efforts of the elders directly concerned, who could curse any of their dependents who continued to fight. They could also put a future curse on anyone who quarreled over certain common rights, such as that of drawing water from a stream between two groups, or walking through a neighboring group to death dances and other rites. These were operative only within the subtribe, which was based upon the subclan. Bonds of common ancestry were invoked to prohibit further fighting, the antithesis of such relationship. There was no set mechanism for the elders to talk peacefully. They merely let it be known that they thought continued fighting pointless. Often mutual sisters' sons would act as intermediaries, and women were also so used. If, however, the fighting groups belonged to different subtribes it was said that the groups continued to fight until the matter was settled and forgotten, after an equal number of persons had been killed on each side. But in any case fighting would give way to necessary economic activity, whether the dispute were settled or not. Subtribal territories were surrounded by land used for grazing and for distant millet fields under shifting cultivation, and much fighting consisted of raids across this land. If one party decided to put down their weapons and go out with hoes and axes to cultivate, the other side would not attack them. "We would see those people were without bows; they carried hoes and went to cultivate. Then we would know they have tired of the fighting and wished to cultivate because perhaps the time is here and the rains are here. Then we would also hoe. And later we would forget that fighting." The need to hoe was used as an excuse to draw fighting to a close without losing face.

In northern Lugbara, especially, fighting within the subtribe could be stopped by the rainmaker chief. He called people together after a lull in the fighting, wearing a cattleskin, and forbade further strife. His words carried the force of a curse.

Following ordinary anthropological usage, we may refer to fighting within the subtribe as feud, and to that between subtribes as warfare. The essential difference is that there was the obligation to settle feuds by peaceful means, whereas there was no such obligation in the case of warfare.

Fighting did not, however, always occur in response to disputes, even in response to homicide. The reaction to this offense is always crucial to the understanding of any judicial system, and in Lugbara it throws a good deal of light on the nature of formal hostility and the structure of the lineage and subclan. There was no social response in terms of force for homicide within the minimal lineage. It was a sin for which there was no humanly awarded punishment. I knew a man who killed his father's brother's son, a "brother" of the same minimal lineage, thinking that he had speared a witch in the guise of a leopard that had been following him. He was drunk at the time and when sober went to the subchief and confessed to what he had done. When I asked what would happen to him, people said: "There are no words. Who will help him now his brother is dead? He will bewail him alone, and die of his brother's blood." A bull was paid on his behalf by his elder (he himself was sent briefly to prison) to his dead "brother's" mother's brother and he inherited his widows. Traditionally nothing further could have happened, because the death could not be avenged. The usual cleansing rites for a homicide did not apply to a fratricide, who commited a deed that was unthinkable and that could never be done deliberately. People said of him, "he is like a *juru*" and feared and avoided him as unnatural; he had broken all bonds of kinship. The beast paid to the victim's mother's brother was not blood money. It was known as "the beast to give (for) the corpse." It was eaten by the group receiving it and not placed in their herd: "Our sister's son would have lived and begotten children, but now his days are cut."

If a fight within the same major lineage led to death the killer gave compensation of two bulls and two cows to the victim's sons, "for them to get wives with," and one bull was also given to his mother's brother.

Beyond the major lineage and section no blood money was payable. Retaliation was made and the situation was of a different order. Close kinship ties were here irrelevant and could be forgotten. A man who killed an enemy—not a mere homicide, but a killing in feud—outside his own major section formally and ceremonially rejoiced and was ritually cleansed by his elder. If it were not done the killer died of "blood" due to the victim's anger, because at this range compensation was not given. Traditionally, if the victim were of a group "far away," that is, of another subtribe, his penis and his right thumb ("with which he shoots people") were cut off and his corpse left to be collected by the women of his lineage, who would not be molested. These parts were placed on a tree, "spiked like (sacrificial) meat" on a branch, and his head was sometimes placed on the path by which he had come. "Truly he was a man, but now we have conquered him." Sometimes penis and thumb were placed in the bundles of sticks called *siriba,* bundles of great magical power kept in the thatch of the owner's hut. It is said that the victim's heart might also be removed and eaten by the killer's lineage. Lugbara did not pride themselves on having been noble fighters—if a man could kill an enemy by stealth and guile he did so. In the accounts I was given, the details of mutilating the corpse and jeering at the discomforted foes were always told with great glee, and clearly this aspect was considered extremely important, as it was the point at which intergroup hostility was realized to its fullest extent.

## CHIEFS, HEADMEN, AND THE ADMINISTRATION OF JUSTICE

Although the Lugbara had no chiefs before the advent of colonial administration, by the 1950s the chiefs had become important poeple and an integral part of Lugbara society. The first chiefs appointed were meant to administer subtribes. But these units were too small to be politically independent and they were amalgamated into counties and subcounties at various times between 1920 and 1950. By 1950, most larger subtribes were administered by subcounty chiefs, and the smaller ones were part of subcounties. By 1950, county and subcounty chiefs were educated men, each with an office, tiled brick house, court and small jail, and with a few police, clerks, and other petty officials. They were members of a local bureaucracy, usually without ties of lineage with the people whom they administered. Up to about 1945 many of the older chiefs had been men from their own chiefdoms; most had been illiterate, and although much respected were unable to cope with many of the problems of modern administration. They were retired, and more educated men were appointed in their places. At the time I was in Lugbara, county and subcounty chiefs were paid career officials, as were the members of their staffs.

Beneath them were parish chiefs and headmen.[2] They were paid only very small salaries, were mostly illiterate and uneducated, and were regarded as "chiefs" by the Lugbara. Parish chiefs were usually responsible for major sections or the smaller subtribes, and headmen were responsible for minor and sometimes major sections. They were almost always drawn from the areas they represented. They had neither courts, offices, nor staff; they did, however, hold informal meetings, which I call moots.

Certain offenses, as I have mentioned, were regarded as criminal offenses and dealt with by a subchief's summons and a hearing at his court, from which appeal

[2]The term "parish" was used in Uganda for a small administrative unit, and lacks the religious connotation of the English "parish."

might be made to a county chief's court. The most prevalent of these offenses was tax evasion. Homicide and rape were also considered criminal offenses. Civil offenses, arising from disputes between individuals, were treated somewhat differently. If the parties to the dispute were both within the small group administered by a headman or a parish chief they usually took it to a moot. Headmen and parish chiefs had no means of enforcing a decision, but brought the dispute into the open and used their powers of persuasion to resolve it and restore peace and friendship. A moot was informal and attended by those who cared to do so; these were usually older men and those known for their wisdom and knowledge of Lugbara tradition and precedent. The aim of a moot was not to punish but to restore the neighborhood ties that had been disrupted by quarrels. If the moot could not do this, the case would be taken to the subchief's court. There the subchief could give verdicts involving punishments of imprisonment, fines, or compensation.

But if the disputants were under the authority of different parish chiefs the case went directly to a subchief's court. In this case each party would first discuss the matter with his own parish chief, who went with him to the court as a sponsor. The parish chief might often plead for him before the subchief. The subchief was impartial, both because he did not have ties of kinship or lineage with the parties before him and because the Lugbara regarded county and subcounty chiefs as representatives of the central administration rather than of themselves; they saw them as *Mundu* ("Europeans"), members of the class known as "New People," rather than as "one of us."

It was noticeable that the chiefs' courts dealt with those disputes that would in the past have been settled by fighting. Disputes that were traditionally settled by peaceful means were in the 1950s dealt with either by elders (if the parties were closely related) or by headmen (if they were just neighbors). From figures that I collected from various subchiefs' court records I found that about 40 percent were in respect to seduction of unmarried girls; about 30 percent were brought by the chiefs themselves for tax evasion or failure to carry out government orders; about 15 percent were for assault, usually arising from marital disputes. In short, chiefship had taken over the role formerly played by feud and warfare.

# 5 / Marriage and Maternal Kinship

## MARRIAGE AND EXOGAMY

Intergroup fighting was intimately connected with relations based on marriage as it was the only sanction for orderly relations between lineages not related by kinship. The myths of the heroes show this connection, and Lugbara themselves stated it quite explicitly.

Marriage in Lugbara was marked by the transfer of bridewealth from the minimal lineage of the bridegroom to that of the bride. By the rules of exogamy that regulated the choice of a wife, a man might not marry a woman of his own clan. Nor might he marry into the major lineage of his mother; this prohibition was inherited for three generations.

The range of permitted marriage was not the same as that of permitted sexual relations. This could be seen particularly on occasions such as death dances, when young men might openly say that they have intercourse with distant clan sisters. This intercourse, which was considered rather dashing by the young men concerned, took place outside the compounds, in the grassland, and could not be followed by conception. If the girl became pregnant, the two were considered to have committed incest, a serious offense that needed ritual purification. A man would not have intercourse with a distant clan sister inside her homestead, however, as this would be tampering with the rights held in her by her father. Neither would he marry her.

The traditional pattern of courtship was for young women to be visited by young men in the special girls' hut built at the edge of the compound of a family cluster. This hut was under the care of an old widow of the lineage, and in it slept the young women and men. An adolescent girl was visited by as many boys as she cared to accept. To accept the same boy too often was considered "greedy" and was ridiculed. The boys entered the hut at dusk and left before dawn. Usually sets of brothers visited sets of sisters. Physical intercourse was not permitted. It was traditionally regarded as a form of rape; the offending boy might be beaten by the girl's brothers and even put to death. By the 1950s, however, intercourse had become common,[1] and a seduction fine of a bull was paid only if the girl became

---

[1]Young men said that they like to "test" a woman to see whether she were likely to make a good wife. If she succumbed to their blandishments she was likely to prove promiscuous and therefore a bad wife, but if she did not, the boys might not wish to visit her. It seemed rather unfair on the young woman.

pregnant. By the time the girl was about fourteen years old she had decided whom she wished to marry. The father of the young man consulted the elder and other senior men of the minimal lineage. If there were no bars of exogamy, the elder went to discuss the matter with the girl's elder. This led to much visiting, during which both sides were perfectly aware of the reasons for this calling, although the actual marriage negotiations might not be opened for some time. At this time the elders carefully addressed one another as *ma agii* ("my friend"), which showed, as Lugbara cynically remarked, that they probably disliked each other in their hearts— "why else call a man your friend?" The visits were accompanied by gifts of beer, which became larger on each occasion, to show good intentions and also to show up the other side's meanness. Finally, negotiations started about the amount of bridewealth and the actual beasts concerned. The word for "to marry" is *je*, the same word used to mean "buy," "exchange," or "barter." It should not be translated as "to buy" in this context, for the simple reason that this translation refers only to the modern economic activity of purchase with money, which was not traditional. But it may be translated as "exchange": the power of procreation and the sexual rights held in the woman by her father and her minimal lineage were transferred to her husband's lineage in return for certain property.

The marriage payments consisted of certain objects. There was first a bull, the "bull of seduction." This bull was the same as that transferred for seduction of an unmarried girl. Lugbara said logically that a husband would in the nature of events seduce his wife, and so this bull had to be transferred. The transfer thus represented the sexual rights in the woman. In theory, if a bull had already been paid for her by a previous lover, one would not have been also transferred by the husband, but I know of no such case, as it would have been regarded as insulting to the girl's family. There were then about seven head of cattle, which represented the pro-creative power of the woman. The "cattle" might in fact be goats, and even money, bicycles, and other goods were known to be transferred instead, although this was unusual and thought improper. If there was later a divorce, the cattle were returned, less one for every child born, the children remaining with the husband. The equivalence of cattle and children was here shown very clearly. Arrows were also transferred. They were a form of currency for use in certain situations, of which this was one. Several hundred arrows were collected from both the father's and mother's kin of the bridegroom, and handed over to the bride's father who in turn distributed them among her paternal and maternal kin. The transfer of arrows marked the establishment of the ties of affinity between the two lineages. Finally, there were gifts of beer given to the girl's mother, to recompense her for the loss of her daughter, to heal her grief, and also to enable her to get a substitute for a few days to help in the home. The beer represented, partly at any rate, the role of the girl as a domestic worker in her mother's home.

There might be a period of several weeks or even months between the agreement in the negotiations and the actual marriage. This period ended with the symbolic death of the bride and her capture by the groom's lineage. The girl covered herself with chalk and ashes and wailed, while her mother and sisters did the same and would sing songs and dance a special women's mourning dance. She was taken from her homestead by her husband and his lineage "brothers," with mock fighting against her brothers; this sometimes became serious, as there was always tension between affinally linked lineages. They were ready to quarrel over the bridewealth and the treatment of the wife at her new home, and there was also resentment at losing a daughter. Her mother was consoled by presents of cloth, beer, and money. It is said that traditionally this took all day, but when I was there it was usually over within an hour or two, and the practice was not always observed. The girl then went to her new home where she and her husband spent several nights and days in a hut alone. There were no public tests for virginity, although the husband's mother was said usually to have made sure that the girl was in fact a virgin; but many Lugbara admitted that by no means all girls were virgins at marriage, and to have public tests and declarations would merely have been embarrassing to everyone. Nonetheless, it was a topic of conversation and interest and was sure to be brought up if there were quarrels later.

A newly married wife "feared" or respected her husband, his father, mother, and brothers. She would sit quietly on the ground when they were present and waited for them to speak before speaking to them herself. She put a mat and a stool down for them when they entered the homestead, and cooked food for them, since "it is their homestead, here." She might not eat with them (although a man with only one wife usually ate with her when they had no visitors and were alone in their hut). A wife of long standing was on easier terms with her husband and might eat with him alone without fearing displeasure from his kin. At first she was shy before her husband's brothers because one of them might later inherit her, and they referred to and addressed her as "our wife."

When the bride became pregnant the marriage became more settled, and when she was a mother of a son it was complete. If she did not become pregnant it was said that the blessing her father had given her on her marriage day, by spitting on her forehead, was not given with a good heart, and visits were made to persuade him to bless her properly. If she did not conceive within six months or so there was usually quarreling and the wife was sent home and the bridewealth demanded back, or a sister might be sent in her place. Although her own lineage would try to blame the matter on the husband's lineage, usually by accusing them of witchcraft, it was generally accepted that barrenness of the wife was the cause. Barrenness and adultery by a wife were grounds for divorce, although adultery was usually first punished by beating. Wives were expected to visit their natal homes regularly, taking gifts and returning with them, and the brothers-in-law were also expected to visit and to behave as friends. A good wife loved her husband, looked after his needs, and after a year or so suggested girls to sleep with him who might later become wives. A good husband loved his wife, did not beat her too much, and treated her exactly equally in every respect with her co-wives. In a polygynous household there was invariably tension between the co-wives, although a senior wife with a strong personality could keep her juniors in check; but the slightest favoritism by the husband would release hostility and quarreling. The fact that there was a word for "favorite wife" (the young one who was favored sexually if not in other ways), which was used as a term of abuse, shows that tension was expected. Co-wives were also said to ensorcell one another, and especially one another's children. However, Lugbara wives appeared to be very free. They visited their kin

*Co-wifes shelling pigeon peas.*

frequently; they might stay away for long periods and were then suspected of adultery, but husbands could do little about it; if they were beaten or mistreated they ran away to their brothers who might themselves come immediately to beat the husband. It was common for wives who ran away to wait until they had a newborn child, and then run home with it so that the baby was a hostage to ensure conciliatory behavior by the husband. About two marriages in ten ended in divorce, the usual reasons being adultery and barrenness on the part of the wives. In a polygynous society of this kind the husband could not himself commit adultery merely by sleeping with other women provided they were themselves unmarried.

However, divorce occurred less frequently after the birth of children than before, especially of male children. When a wife had had a child who had survived the first few years of life,[2] her husband's lineage transferred a beast to her father's lineage, and this marked the acceptance of the wife by the husband's lineage as a mother of their children. After that, her position in the household eased greatly. She needed no longer to observe the formal rules of avoidance in private (although she would continue to do so in public) and her mother-in-law would cease to see her as a rival for her son's affection and would accept her as an ally, as a fellow-wife living in a strange lineage home.

[2]At the time of my stay, one child in three died during the first year of life.

If a woman were divorced, she returned to the care of her natal lineage. She was in a difficult position. Divorced women were usually regarded as flighty and difficult to control. They led lives free of many of the irksome duties of a wife, and although they were often almost disowned by their own lineage if they did not remarry quickly, many women preferred this status to that of a wife subject to domestic discipline and having to respect her affines. Nonetheless, these women were few and had a generally low status. Lugbara values decreed that a woman should be married and have children—it was said that "the work of women is to bear children"—and only those women who were barren became permanently divorced. They often acquired position of a different order by becoming traders or pot makers, or, if they were able, became diviners.

A woman who was past menopause became a "big woman." She was in some contexts regarded socially as a man, and could take part in ritual, share her husband's portion of sacrificial meat, and even take his position in some lesser rites if he were absent. She might represent him at oracle seances and could offer certain sacrifices, and when he died she might "guard" his shrines. The curse of such an old woman was greatly feared and she could exercise considerable authority over her children and other kin.

A widow was inherited by one of her husband's successors in the lineage, usually either a brother or a son by another wife. After the period of mourning, she lived alone in her hut and would be visited at night by as many of the possible inheritors as she might wish to accept. When she decided to stay with a particular one, she handed him a hoe one morning as a sign of her approval of him as her pro-husband. Lugbara said that the "minds of widows are strong" and that they enjoyed their power of choice. The new union was not a new marriage but a continuation of the old one. Children born to a widow after inheritance regarded the pro-husband as their social and legal father. This was the institution of widow inheritance and not the true levirate.[3]

An old widow might refuse to be inherited and choose to be protected by one of her own sons, who would build her a hut where she would eke out a rather pathetic existence until she died. However, a man regarded his mother with great respect, and although old and poor she might hold considerable status and be treated with overt respect by those around her.

## KIN BY MARRIAGE

For the Lugbara, marriage was not merely a union between two individuals but one between two lineages and two clusters of kinsfolk. By the rule of exogamy, these lineages had to be unrelated, or only distantly related (people of the same clan did in fact marry if the tie was a remote one). Throughout a marriage the ties of a woman

[3]Neither did the Lugbara practice ghost-marriage or woman-marriage, institutions frequently found in association with the levirate (Evans-Pritchard 1951). When I told Lugbara of these Nuer practices they were amazed and scornful, asking: "What kind of fools are these? When a man dies, he dies, his body rots. . . . We are as we are here, we are not like those people in the Sudan, indeed."

to her natal kin were remembered and were important. I was soon aware of the sense of responsibility people had for their sisters and daughters married elsewhere, and regular visits were made to see that they were well.

A marriage created new ties of kinship between the two groups. The first was that of affinity, marked by the transfer of arrows, as I have mentioned. The second, which was made by the birth of a child, was that of maternal kinship between the child and his mother's lineage. The tie of affinity was centered on the relationship between the brothers-in-law *(otu),* who were expected to regard one another as equals and friends, though they were usually, at first at any rate, suspicious of each other. The wife's brother might resent having lost a sister, and her husband often resented having given what he considered too much bridewealth. Much depended on the wife's behavior and the husband's treatment of her: if she soon bore children and was a good wife, and if he treated her well, the brothers-in-law usually did respect and like each other. But I knew many brothers-in-law who regarded each other as virtual enemies and who waited for opportunities to score against one another and to shout abuse and brawl.

When a child was born, the tie of maternal kinship was created between the child and its maternal kin. This, unlike that of affinity, was a tie of "blood," and a very intimate and important one for Lugbara. A man regarded his sister's child "like his own child. Are they not of one blood? Is not his mother my own sister?" The sister's child knew that he could expect affection and help from the mother's brother throughout his life. As I have said earlier, a man would turn to his mother's brother for land or assistance if he quarreled with his own family. The mother's brother always assisted him, thus enabling him to score against his sister's son's father, who was his own brother-in-law.

At the basis of the relationship between brothers-in-law and that of a man and his sister's son was a resentment at having lost a sister to another lineage. Lugbara stressed this, saying that if only the sister had been born a man she would have begotten children for her own lineage, but because the Creator Spirit made her a woman, she had to bear children for another group. Her children were nonetheless very close to her own kin, who protected them; this was continued after their death, when the sister's son set special shrines for his mother's brother's ghost.

The ambivalence in the relationship between mother's brother and sister's son is typical, of course, in patrilineal societies. In Lugbara it was expressed formally in two ways. One was that the kinship term used was a reciprocal one, *adro;* although of different generations, they were formally made equal in status by each using the same term of address toward the other. The other was by "joking" between a man and his mother's brother, but even more between him and his mother's brother's wife. She was called *o'da,* which was both a kin term and also the verb "to joke." "Joking" took the form of insults between them when they met, most references in the insults being sexual. The "joking" was obligatory, and it was thought that a man who did not joke would later get scabies as a punishment for ignoring correct kinship behavior. Lugbara said that a man would insult his mother's brother's wife because if he (the sister's son) had been born a member of his mother's lineage he might later have inherited that particular woman when she became a widow. A man could take food and other things from his mother's brother's compound ("It should have been his food, but his mother was born a woman and not a man"), and the mother's brother's wife was a form of property also: he could not take her as he did food, but insulted her instead. Lugbara said, "You respect your mother's brother's wife but you treat her like a 'thing' also." To insult her was a way of making the distinction between the two lineages, for to use "joking" insults to a member of one's own lineage would lead to immediate fighting and probable mystical punishment.

The ties between individual kin through women were recognized also between their lineages. The collective forms of the kinship terms were used to apply to them: *adropi* (mother's brother's people) and *otupi* (wife's brother's people). They could refer to one's mother's family cluster, to her minor or major lineage, and even to her subclan. *Adropi* was used to refer to the distant groups that were known to be in some way related by maternal kinship. In theory there was a joking relationship recognized with such groups also, but the "joking" was mild. Any obscenity of the kind used with the true mother's brother and his wife would be thought out of place and resented.

# 6 / Spirit and the Ancestors

## OFFENSES AND SINS

I have mentioned that when people were related by close kinship the principal sanctions for proper behavior between them were religious. By this I mean that the Lugbara believed these sanctions were brought into operation by the Creator Spirit, ancestors and their ghosts, or various kinds of spirit; with these agents might be included witches and sorcerers, for although they were thought to be ordinary living men and women their powers were believed to come from Spirit and to be of a different order from the skills and abilities of normal people. In the next two chapters I shall discuss certain aspects of Lugbara religion from this point of view, to show how religious beliefs and practices acted as means of controlling social behavior.

The lineage was the basic Lugbara social group, inasmuch as almost all social relations were conceived in lineage terms. For Lugbara the dead were as much members of the lineage as the living, and as its senior members they were respected and their wishes obeyed. Respect was the basis of ideal behavior toward both living and dead senior men, and provided that juniors respected seniors and women respected men, Lugbara considered that the well-being of the lineage and community would be assured. It was only when men ceased to respect their seniors that things went wrong and the various social sanctions I have mentioned had to be brought into play.

We may distinguish hostility between groups that was expressed in feud and warfare and that expressed by other means. Violence was the antithesis of correct behavior between close kin. A group of kin would not resolve its disputes by such means, especially when it was a small group with a single elder who had authority within it. I have said that where mutually recognized authority, sanctioned by appeal to common ghosts, broke down, self-help was used in its place. The converse was that the resort to self-help destroyed the recognition of common authority and representation. When two closely related lineages resorted to violence it was a sign that their formerly recognized common authority no longer existed.

Disputes about trespass, assault, disobedience of elders' authority, and so on, occured at all levels of the lineage, although they might be settled differently. The minimal lineage recognized the internal domestic authority of the elder; wider segments did not. But the major lineage had other means that minimized the risk of overt hostility. One was that it was exogamous: it might not be the widest exogamous segment of the subclan, but the prohibition of intermarriage within it was rigidly maintained, whereas that beyond might occasionally be broken and the group split into two. This did not occur frequently, but any subclan had a few cases within the last generation or two. Within this lineage, however, sexual relations (as apart from marriage) were regarded as true incest; beyond it Lugbara accepted them as taking place but unless followed by pregnancy or too flagrantly obvious it was unlikely that either the living or the dead would take much notice. But incest within the lineage was thought to be followed by mystical sanctions sent by the dead and by Spirit. Adultery within this segment was also sinful, being a breach of close fraternal relations (unless performed at the request of an impotent or absent husband). Beyond it adultery was followed by fighting or compensation. It was also the group within which homocide was defined as fratricide, for which there was no humanly awarded punishment. Assault, especially if against an older man, was also more of a sin within this range than if beyond it; the latter led to counterassault, the former to mystical sanctions being brought into play. All these offenses within this segment were in the nature of sins, their sinfulness lying in their being expressions of the rejection of true values of patrilineal kinship. At this range sanctions for orderly conduct were mystical, to do with the ghosts and ancestors. Accusations of witchcraft also occurred as substitutes or replacements for overt violence. Relations with more distantly related lineages were sanctioned by the feud. This was also the range to which personal terms of kinship were used.

Most offenses within the lineage, especially incest and fratricide, were called by the term *ezata*. *Eza* is to "destroy" or "spoil," and *ezata* is "destruction" or "destroying"; it was given to me once as "the deed that destroys good words," and a Christian pastor translated it for me as "sin." It was said of a man who committed incest, adultery, or who persistently assaulted and disobeyed his close agnates that he was "a man with sin." It was contrasted with *yeta onzi* ("bad deeds"), which did not need to be concerned with lineage values. But it was not so much the intrinsic nature of the offense as the degree of closeness between offender and victim that was significant. Sins were mystically punished, by the dead and by Spirit. "Bad deeds" were penalized by human response, although the dead and Spirit might also enter into the affair.

There were several other categories of relationship for which there were recognized sanctions. The individual relations between people who were kin but of different lineages were sanctioned by various curses, of which the most feared was that by a man's mother or grandmother (who were, of course, not of his lineage). There were also sicknesses brought by maternal ghosts for breaches of proper behavior by a man to his mother's brother's people. There were the relations between neighbors, controlled by fear of ostracism and witchcraft and sorcery. All the offenses concerned with these relationships were "bad deeds," rather than sins.

## SPIRIT AND THE NATURE OF MAN

Before discussing the cult of the dead, something should be said about the nature of man and Spirit.[1] Lugbara regarded Spirit as an all-pervasive power that stood outside men and beyond their control. It was omnipotent and timeless, and could

[1]In Middleton 1960a I used the term God for what I now prefer to call Spirit.

create and destroy men and send them various sicknesses, disasters, and punishments as well as health and prosperity. Spirit was both good and evil. Spirit as a creator was known as *Adroa 'ba o' bapiri* (Spirit the creator of men), *Adroa onyiru* (good Spirit) or *Adroa 'bua* (Spirit in the sky). Spirit was invisible and "in the wind," and was not personalized, because Spirit created persons and it could hardly therefore be a person itself. Linguistically the form *Adroa* was the diminutive, since it was thought to be remote from men and did not come into direct contact with them.

Besides the transcendent aspect of Spirit in the sky, there was also the immanent form on the surface of the world. This was known as *Adro,* the diminutive form of which is *Adroa.* This aspect of Spirit was thought to have the form of a tall man, white in color, cut in half down the middle, and hopping about on its one leg. It lived in streams, bushland, and on mountains, and if seen would kill the person who glimpsed it. It was often known as *Adro onzi* (evil Spirit), and was greatly feared.[2] This aspect of Spirit came into direct contact with men, and could harm them in many ways. *Adro* also possessed girls and gave them the power of divination. *Adro* was said to have children, *adroanzi* ("*Adro*-children"), who were spirits of various kinds that lived in streams, hills, and trees; they also guarded rain groves. They had the form of small men and women, and could become visible, but a person who saw them would die. *Adroa, Adro,* and the *adroanzi* were found throughout Lugbara. In addition, each clan had its own *adro*-spirit, a manifestation of the power of Spirit that was concerned in the original genesis of each clan. Clans were linked together in this way, as well as having their separate ancestors. There were no rites associated with Spirit, except for certain prayers made to it at times of famine or disaster. Spirit came into contact with the living by sending sicknesses and disasters, and for them to contact it they would use diviners, prophets, or other persons who could communicate with it and who could interpret its various manifestations in the form of sickness, lightning, and epidemics.

When people died, they ceased to be "people of the world outside" and became "people who have died" or "people in the earth." They were still "people" or "persons" *('ba),* that is, human beings with social and moral responsibility, as contrasted to "things" *(afa)* such as clients, babies, and young women, none of whom possesed social responsibility. The dead were said to live somewhere beneath the surface of the world, but people did not know exactly what their life was like. The belief in an afterlife was shadowy and unimportant, and there were no beliefs in heaven or hell nor any rewards after death for offenses or good deeds while alive. "Our ancestors" were benevolent and wished well for their descendents, whom they protected and guided, but punished for sins. Although a dead person's character and personality were remembered for a few years, he or she was not regarded as malevolent after death even if so regarded while alive. Ancestors were thought to be aware of what went on among their living kin, and discussed them among themselves. It was said that they liked to say: "Now our child gives us food, and we are glad." To give food was a sign of close kinship.

A living person had certain elements. He or she had first a body, which became

---

[2]One of the older-fashioned terms for a European was *Adro,* because Europeans are white and were believed to eat the people they took to hospitals and prisons.

a corpse when dead and rotted away in a few years; it was unimportant and "goes nowhere" after death. When alive a body contained breath, which at death went no one knew where. Breath was a sign of life but had no great importance in itself. More important were certain invisible and spiritual elements: the *orindi*, the *adro*, and the *tali*. Of these the most important was the *orindi*, which I translate as "soul." The soul was said to be in the heart, and was the element that made a man act responsibly as a social being and member of a lineage. At death it left the body and went to Spirit in the sky; later it was contacted by a diviner and returned to earth where it lived at a shrine set for it. It was aware of what went on among the living, and could in some mystical manner communicate with certain of the living and could send sickness to living sinners. When back in the shrine it became known as *ori*, which I translate as "ghost." Any dead person, man, woman, or child, became an ancestor *(a'bi)*, but only certain of these became ghosts. "Ancestors" were all a man's dead kinsfolk, and although no one could relate the names of all their ancestors they nonetheless knew that they had lived and that after death they were somewhere in the earth beneath. But only those whose souls had been given shrines were ghosts. A child rarely became a ghost, because his soul was small, and the same applied to most women. It was men who left sons behind to place shrines for them who became ghosts. In effect, of course, this meant that only those ancestors who were remembered in genealogies were also ghosts. An ancestor who became a ghost did not thereby cease being an ancestor, but was rather an ancestor who in death was known to be responsible toward his dead kin; and this was expressed by his being given a shrine at which sacrifices were made to him.

After death the soul of a man might be seen by his living kin as a specter *(atri)*, which was an omen that he had died unhappily and that reparation of some kind should be made to him. Usually contact was made by a diviner, and the wishes of the dead man satisfied. He then rested content and a shrine was later made to his name. It was sometimes also said that the shadow was a form of the soul, but this belief was unimportant, except that witches could harm a victim by treading on a person's shadow.

The other elements were the *adro* and *tali*. I need not discuss them at length. *Adro* was put into the body at birth or conception (it was not known which) by Spirit. It was a sign of humans' divine creation, and can be translated as "spirit." After death it left the body and went off into the bushland, where it became one of the *adroanzi* or spirits of the water, hills, or trees. The *tali* was the element that enabled someone to have influence over others, and it increased in power with age. After death it left the body and lived in a shrine where all the *tali* of past members of the lineage were. *Tali* was a word used for any manifestation of the power of Spirit, such as a place where lightning has struck, or a mystical power such as rainmaking or divination.

## DEATH AND BURIAL

Death marked the beginning of an elaborate *rite de passage*, for both dead persons and for their living kin. The mortuary rites of Lugbara were the only rites or ceremonies that attracted large numbers of people, and were highly important in Lugbara society. Almost every other rite was the concern of a small lineage and neighborhood only, but the mortuary rites of an important man might attract people from neighboring subtribes and last for days or even weeks: I knew cases in which they were not completed for over a year. At death a person's physical body was disposed of and forgotten, and those elements that did not become ancestor and ghost went to the domain of Spirit, either in the sky or in the bushland. Ancestors were important only to their living kin, in particular, members of their lineage; they had no significance to other people. A dead person had relations with both living and dead kin; Lugbara knew little about the latter relations, but the former were modeled on those he or she had had with the living while alive. At death the kinship status of the dead person remained, but other aspects of the social personality were extingushed.

The corpse was buried with certain objects that represented its former status as a man, woman, or child, and with certain objects associated with any status he or she may have acquired outside the lineage. With a man were buried his quiver, his favorite drinking gourd, and his elder's stool if he had been an elder. These objects symbolized the positions he had held during his lifetime: the quiver that of a young man who was a warrior and hunter, the drinking gourd that of the mature man who drank and talked with his kin and neighbors, and the stool that of the elder. In addition, if he had become an oracle operator he was buried with the rubbing-stick and pots he used for the boiling-water oracle. With a woman were buried her beads (which represent her position as a girl and later as a sexually active female), the three fire stones of her hearth ("the stones where she cooked food for her husband"), and the smaller of the two grinding stones with which she had ground flour; these last two represented her status as wife and mother in her husband's lineage. The grinding stone was that which she had actually held while grinding, the one she had chosen herself from the rounded pieces of granite in the stream bed. The larger, lower grinding stone was not vested with her personality as was this upper stone, and passed to her daughter. Her pots, gourds, and other household utensils were broken by her brother, who also scattered the grain from her granary over the compound and pulled the thatch from her hut roof. This was done "because these are her own things, but are little": she had made them but her personality was not in them as it was in the other objects. Both men and women were buried with beans, simsim, and heads of eleusine, the three traditional staple crops of the Lugbara, about which there were myths that told of their being tilled by the heroes (other crops were later importations). The burial of these objects and foodstuffs was in no way in preparation for any kind of journey to the land of the dead. Lugbara stated this quite explicitly and said they were put with the corpse "because he would have eaten them. Now who will eat them? Let us pour them over the corpse." For a woman, then, her brother (her closest kinsman) destroyed her possessions. The objects buried with her symbolized her status as a woman, wife, and mother, and after death it was her status as an ancestress that remained significant in her son's lineage, not that of a wife as such. She was buried in her husband's compound, not taken back to her natal home, if she died where she was married.

The corpse of a child was buried with the little basket that was used to cover its head when being carried on its mother's back, and with a small gourd used to contain the simsim oil with which it was cleansed.

Other possessions were inherited. They were primarily the dead person's livestock, and the stones of the shrines that a man had set up himself. Both men and women could acquire their own livestock during their lives, by working or trading, and these were their individual property. Livestock were "things of the lineage" and in theory they might be used only for bridewealth or sacrifice, never merely killed for meat.

The grave as such was not important, and was soon forgotten. An adult man was buried inside his first wife's hut, in the center of the floor. The grave was from four to six feet deep, with a recess in the center of the floor in which the corpse was laid, with legs straight and right hand under the head. The head was placed in the direction of either Mount Liru or Mount Eti, according to whether the dead person was High or Low Lugbara. A papyrus sleeping mat was placed at the bottom of the grave, and then the hide of one of the dead man's bulls killed for the purpose by his brothers. The corpse was also usually wrapped in white cloth. This and the washing of the corpse was done by his lineage sisters, chosen from the major lineage and of the same generation as the dead man. The grave was dug and the corpse buried by "mother's brothers," "because he was our child, there." Over the corpse in its recess were placed granite slabs to prevent earth from falling onto it. The grave was then filled in with earth and a cairn of stones raised on top of it; after a few years this was moved and the site cultivated. Women were buried in their huts likewise, except they lay on their left side and no cattleskin was placed beneath the body. Children were buried in the same way, either in the mother's hut or in the hut doorway.[3] A miscarriage of a fetus of over three months counted as the death of a child, and mourning and burial were as for those of a child.

Elders and very senior women (those who were the senior sisters of men who became elders, and so who would have themselves been elders had they not been born women) were buried outside the huts, in the compound, usually near the chief wife's granary, under which were the ghost shrines. The burial was the same as for other people, but a thatched roof three or four feet high was often built over the grave and a barkcloth tree planted at its head. They were buried outside "because they are big" and thus feared. If buried inside the huts their widows' bodies would become "bad." Wailing for an elder began when his cattle lowed after his death. A rainmaker was also buried outside the compound on the edges of the bushland, but whereas an ordinary person was buried to wailing and dancing, a rainmaker was buried in silence, at night, lest he turn into a leopard at the burial. Dead lepers were exposed in the bushland, without burial rites being performed for them. They were believed to have acquired the disease by being cursed by their kin or by committing incest, and were therefore said to be beyond the ties of kinship. The same applied to persons killed by lightning or epidemics, both of which were regarded as actions of Spirit.

The burial was mainly the affair of the immediate lineage kin, especially those of the same generation, and of mother's brothers only. Other kin entered the

---

[3]Father Ramponi states that twins were buried in double-mouthed pots, but I have been unable to confirm this (see E. Ramponi, 1937).

compound to watch and wail, and they also wailed and danced outside the compound; I describe the dancing below.

The dead person's mother, mother's sisters, and widows did not touch the corpse. They wailed loudly and covered their heads and bodies with dust and earth, and they might throw themselves on the ground and roll about in the ashes of the fire of the compound, which was put out at death. The mother and the widows did not remove the dust and ashes, nor shave their heads or wash until the end of the period of mourning. Both mourning and the ashes used were called *uri* ("fear" or "respect"). These women had special cries of mourning, which were different from those used by the lineage sisters, which were in their turn different from those used by other kin and by neighbors.

Mourning affected only the immediate kin of the dead person, and especially a widow, who entered into seclusion until the end of the mourning period. During this time they lived in a small hut built for the purpose, and might neither wash nor shave their heads, which remained whitened with finely powdered ashes. Other members of the immediate family and sisters' children were not secluded but did not shave their heads for the same period. They wore ashes on their faces for four days if the dead person were a man, or three if a woman.

The lineage sisters who touched the corpse were regarded as ritually unclean. After the burial they washed in the nearest stream before they mixed with other people, and they were not allowed to oil their bodies (a sign that the pollution had not finally been removed). The mother's brothers who prepared the grave were not so polluted. They merely washed and rejoined the dancers afterward. This washing was different from that of the lineage sisters, who went formally to the stream together, often under the direction of a diviner, but the mother's brothers regarded their lustration as something rather everyday.

All other kin who attended the burial shaved their heads, especially those who actually entered the compound. Lugbara said this was done to be "clean," and thus not harmed by the corpse. They might also put ashes on their heads, but usually only on their foreheads and not over the entire face. Women, however, did not wear fresh leaves as apparel, but wore those of the day before. The compound was not swept, and was left dirty until after the end of the period of mourning.

Once the corpse was buried, the process of changing the dead person's status from that of a living to a dead kinsman started. A dead kinsman was both respected and feared, in much the same way as a living man when he became senior in lineage and family position. On the whole the dead were regarded as beneficent, the origins of law and order and custom. Their ability to send sickness to their living descendants was part of their role as the guardians of morality, and it was accepted that they did not do so wantonly or without adequate reason. But they were also feared. This was true especially of the newly dead, since it was not known what grudges they might hold toward their living kin at the time they died. A man who knew he was about to die called his close lineage kin to him and spoke his last words, in which he was said to designate his lineage successor and to bring into the open any grudges that he might hold. In fact, the living tended to interpret the last words of a dying man as they themselves felt best for the lineage. Immediately after death the soul went to the place of Spirit in the sky, outside the control of living men, and it was at this time that any resentment toward them by the living would be expressed openly, and they might haunt the living as specters to show that they had died with grudges. Once the dead became full ancestors and ghosts, any resentment toward them was ideally not permitted, since by then it should have been dispersed by the diviner contacting the soul. The ambivalent attitude toward a senior kinsman was largely an aspect of the relationship to him as a known individual, which lessened after his death as the memory of him faded.

Resentment might, however, be expressed overtly at his burial. The death of an important man was followed by a period when many of the obligations of kinship were temporarily in abeyance. This period was marked by permitted license in behavior between kin, and by the non-sweeping of the lineage compounds.

At the burial the dead man's successor and other men of the minimal lineage concerned spoke of him and recounted the "words of the ancestors." They brought certain sacred leaves, which were associated with Spirit, dipped them in water, and placed them on the ground. If that evening a jackal or other night creature defecated on them they knew that the dead man had died with a "bad" heart, but if there was no excrement on the leaves the next morning it was a sign that he had died content and by the will of Spirit, about which he could not complain. This was done for all men who left children, and for old women, but not for young women and children. Before the grave was closed the lineage kin stood around it, addressed the dead man, and expressed any overt resentment toward him. One such address that I heard included the words:

> Now you are dead. You fear now. . . . It is good that you fear. . . . You have begotten children and done many things. . . . Now you are dead, like a pot that is broken. If your heart is bad, then tomorrow we shall see. . . . Now you are dead and your words are little. . . .

At the burial also a bull or goat had to be given to the deceased's own true mother's brother. This was the "corpse beast." If the deceased were a woman, her agnates were given a beast as well, known also as "corpse beast." The burial did not take place until this had been done, for until they had accepted it, the mother's brother and, if a woman, her lineage kin, were not satisfied as to the cause of death. If they were not satisfied, they usually suspected witchcraft. The dead man would then return to haunt his lineage, or a woman to haunt her husband's lineage.


## DEATH DANCES

So far I have mentioned some of the events that were connected with the change of a person's status from a living to a dead member of the lineage. But he or she had been at the center of a network of ties between lineages and groups of kin. At death there was a rearrangement of these ties. These realignments were of relationships between the minimal lineage and other groups and were made at death dances.

The dances started after the death, usually immediately after the burial. There were two sets of dances, the *ongo* and the *abi*. *Ongo* was the generic term for "dance," and these dances were highly elaborated. There were many variations but always two main dances: the "wailing dance" and the "leaping dance." Each consisted of several distinct dances with their own songs telling of the dead person's life and way of dying. As in most Lugbara songs, there was much bitter and sarcastic allusion to the failings of other lineages, and so there was a good deal of airing of grievances and thereby disposing of them.[4]

Both men and women danced, although the main dances in the center of the arena—usually a cleared space outside the compound—were done mostly by men only, the women being on the periphery. Much beer would be drunk, and because men carried spears and arrows there was often fighting. Women carried wands, and senior women, those who were the first born of sets of brothers and sisters and therefore "like men," might carry quivers. In the dances men stood by generation, not by lineage or family. The team consisted of the men of a lineage. Lineages that entered the arena first thereby showed their seniority over other lineages, and fighting often occurred as they jostled to take their position as a previous dance ended. There might also be brawling among the dancers themselves: those of the same generation danced side by side, leaping up and down, and to jolt one's neighbor could lead to argument and fighting. These dances were not solemn occasions. Because dances might continue for days and nights at a stretch, with the drums never stopping,[5] many people were soon in a trancelike condition and normally expected behavior would be relaxed. Lugbara recognized this, saying: "Death has destroyed the words, a big man is dead and we are like children with no one to help us." This behavior was expressed in many ways: by the fluidity of lineage relationships as seen in the jostling for seniority and the fighting; by the normally forbidden seduction of clan-sisters by young men, an accepted piece of bravado that was said "to show young men who are their clan-sisters" (the implication being that with lineage ties in temporary disarray people would forget their relationships); and sometimes in the reversal of sexual roles, usually by young men wearing women's leaves as apparel or women leading men's dance teams.

While the dancing was going on, couples ran out of the throng of watchers to the outskirts of the arena. There the man cried his *cere* call[6] and shot arrows into the bush (or mimicked doing so) and the woman called her *cere*. There was no expected relationship between the pair, except that they were never husband and wife; they might be lineage or other kin, or merely close friends. The expressed purpose of this action was that it "showed" other lineages that the pair wished to avenge the death. It was done only for adult men.

I soon saw that death dances were of great importance. They were the occasions for the greatest coming together of kinsfolk. There was little ceremonial or ritual at birth and marriage, and no initiation ritual. Large dances were said to have been held in the past at the first harvests in the year, but they were smaller than big death dances. Other dances, *koro* and *walangaa* ("dances of play"), were recent in-

---

[4]Lugbara themselves said that when a grievance was openly expressed anyone who later took it up would become ashamed and lose face.

[5]There were usually three drums; the "child," the "wife," and the "grandmother," and players changed over from time to time without stopping the beat.

[6]The *cere* was a long, high-pitched falsetto whooping cry. Every adult man and woman had his or her own (to which words were fitted). They were traditionally called for help and at dances, and men called them when coming home drunkenly from beer parties, so that they could be recognized in the dark, and also to show that they were "big." It was a deep insult to cry another person's *cere* except at the one occasion when a man's heir cried the dead man's call immediately after his death.

troductions, and the traditional *nyambi* dance of women, danced at a bride's leaving her natal home, attracted only a small audience. But death dances were the cause for excitement and interest over a wide area, and the continual drumming and singing were audible for miles.

The *ongo* dances were performed immediately after the death; those for an important man might last for a week, those for a young man, a woman, or a child for only a day or so and be attended by only a few close kin. At various periods afterward, usually during the following harvest season when plenty of food and beer was easily available, the dances known as *abi* were held. These occurred at odd times as groups of kin visited, and might continue for up to a year, and even longer for very important men. The occasions and the atmosphere at them were very different. The *ongo* were performed by close kin of the same lineage, the maternal kin, and groups that had married women of the dead man's lineage. They came "to dance the death dance" and "to wail," and brought arrows that were given to the dead man's close lineage kin. It was said, "You always give to where you get your wife," and these arrows were a continuation of the bridewealth payments made earlier. They were given to "help" the dead man's lineage; they might be accompanied by gifts of food, and the visitors were formally given food and beer. The *abi* dances were performed by groups of visiting affines who came "to rejoice." They came from those lineages that had supplied women as wives to the lineage of the dead man, and were given arrows in their turn. The "rejoicing" was because by paying respect and receiving arrows they showed that the tie of affinity had been reaffirmed after being weakened by the death of the person who had been the link between the two lineages.

The death dances were, as I have said, the occasions for the recognition of the rearrangement of ties between kin after a death. The ties that were formally stressed were those that cut across lineage affiliation. Although groups came to dance as lineages, it was the kinship relationship of them as a category (lineage, maternal, or affinal kin) that was stressed and not their lineage identity as such. People said, "Here are our mothers' brothers who come to dance," rather than using the name of the lineage. Within the teams of dancers, men of the same generation would dance together, and generations would succeed each other.

Death dances should have been times of peace and amity, but they were frequently occasions of fighting and quarreling, as lineages competed for recognition of their seniority. This lack of any firm or generally accepted genealogical seniority between related lineages, and of any superior authority to determine such seniority, ran through much of Lugbara ritual. It was a point of continual discussion and competition, and a great deal of the cult of the dead was concerned with this competition. Death, especially of an elder, was a time when the segmentation of his lineage was likely, the succession to eldership providing a precipitating cause. The realignment between lineage segments was decided inside the dying man's hut during his last words, and later at the dances when it was formally stressed that lineage differences should be forgotten and generation unity stressed. What happened was that the lineage alignment that had been accepted hitherto, and had been maintained by the dead elder's authority, might now no longer be accepted, and lineages struggled to claim seniority over their fellow lineages at the time of uncertainty.

I return to this point later, because the competition for relative status at death dances was not an isolated phenomenon. It continued between deaths in the form of competition for ancestral favor in the rites of the ghost cult, and also, of course, in secular alliances in feuds and court cases. Death dances provided one opportunity for attempting to get public acceptance of relative status, since these dances were the occasion of such wide gatherings of kin. I have considered them, briefly, before discussing ritual proper; but they may be understood as providing a climax, as well as a beginning, to competition waged between heads of families and lineages during the lifetime of the senior man.

## CONTACTING THE SOUL

There remained only to bring the soul of the dead person into a permanent relationship with the living, a relationship that was centered physically upon shrines erected for it. This was done by three acts: contacting the soul "in the sky," settling any grudges and anger it might have had toward the living, and building the shrine for it. These could all be done at the same time, or spread out over several weeks or even months. Much depended on the dead person's status—the higher, the more likely was the process to be spread out—and on whether the living kin had the food and beer needed for these rites (it depended therefore to some extent on the time of year).

The soul, especially that of a senior man, was contacted either if sickness came upon one of his kinsmen and an oracle stated that it was sent by the recently dead soul, or if someone dreamed about the dead person or saw him as a specter. Contact was made by a diviner, a woman who had the mystical power to speak with the dead soul. She discovered whether or not it had died contentedly or with grudges against the living. If the former, the diviner erected a shrine, but if the latter, the grudge had first to be settled. Later the chief heir of the dead person erected a shrine to his ghost when he first made a sacrifice to it.

Shrines were of many kinds. The principal shrines were those erected for a ghost of an ancestor. They were known in most of Lugbaraland as *orijo* ("ghost house") and consisted of pieces of granite formed into a rough house or shelter and placed under the chief wife's granary; they might take the form of a miniature hut with a thatched roof. A ghost did not have merely a single shrine, but could have several, one in each of its patrilineal descendants' compounds. A ghost shrine was named after its incumbent. It was not thought to dwell in the shrine but rather to use it as a place where it might receive sacrificial food and beer from those of its descendants who lived in that particular compound.

There were many types of shrines set for the dead. The ghost shrines were the most important, because it was the ghosts who most often sent sickness. Shrines were also set for the ancestors as ancestors, that is, including those ancestors who had not become ghosts because they had left no sons behind; for the ghosts of mothers' brothers; for women of the lineage; and for many kinds of spirits. There is not the space in this account to give details of them all (Middleton 1960a, Chap. II).

# 7 / The Cult of the Dead

Certain offenses, those I call sins, were followed by mystical sanctions and by sacrifice to the ghosts. These sanctions were put into operation and controlled by living people who had the power both to interpret the actions and motives of the dead and to intercede with them to withdraw the sanctions when the time was appropriate.

Lugbara recognized that a lineage segmented, and that quarreling and disputes were signs of incipient segmentation. Yet ideally there should be peace within it. Kin would quarrel, but the ideal of kinship was peaceful cooperation for the common good. Men were ambitious and wanted power, but for a man to be accused of personal ambition was to label him a deviant from the ideal, a man who thought more of his own position than that of the welfare of the members of the lineage. A lineage vested authority in its elder; anyone else who tried to exercise power within the group threatened the elder's authority and therefore the well-being of the lineage. Undelegated power and authority could not both be exercised within the same unit by different people. The problem here, of course, was to permit diffferent people to hold ambitions that might be mutually incompatible. The head of a family within the family cluster had the duty of pressing the claims of his own family's members against those of the other families. He was expected to do this and his dependents would complain if he did not. Yet from the viewpoint of the total family cluster he should not do this but should discuss matters in amity with his fellow heads of families, and the head of a family frequently found himself in a position of conflict. The ideal of the elder's behavior was that he should be quiet, dignified, slow in decision, and ready to act in union with his "brothers," the elders of other minimal lineages. The unity of the lineage was the ideal. But not all elders and senior men observed the ideal; younger men did so still less, and indeed in the more distant past would not have been admired as warriors if they had. There was the feeling that younger men were more disruptive, because they lacked the social maturity and experience of elders. The expected behavior (but not perhaps the ideal) of younger men thus in fact fitted the position in which they found themselves, that of heads of junior families, exhorted by their own dependents to gain benefits for these families but subject to the overall unity of the lineage and the authority of its elder. A young man who showed "slowness" was pointed out in old men's discussions as a man of promise, but he might find himself despised by his equals. The expected behavior of men of different levels of seniority in the lineage thus differed: a "youth" looked out for himself among his fellow youths but should obey his seniors; a "big youth," who had married and started a family, should fight for the rights of his wives in land and other resources, but had also to recognize his responsibilities to the wider group; the "men behind" were the heads of joint families, usually of equal generation to elders but debarred from eldership by the vagaries of birth and genealogy; and, finally, the elders exercised authority for the good of all and had to forget their simultaneous position as heads of their own families, which were only units of the lineages of which they were the heads. These levels of seniority were not formal, and there was no initiation into any of them.

In a similar way, the relations between minimal lineages and the family clusters formed around them, and therefore between their elders, were expected to be both of competition to maintain their separate rights and of unity and alliance in which mutual interests were paramount. An elder once said to me: "Elders often quarrel among themselves like young men; we are men and all men have bad hearts. But the ancestors do not quarrel among themselves." Although it was often said that the dead did in fact quarrel, in this context the meaning was clear. The "elder" who really joined under his own authority two related lineages was an ancestor.

Lugbara thus recognized fairly explicitly that divisive phases in the history of a lineage corresponded to, and were expressed in, quarrelsomeness and ambition on the part of heads of segments, whereas cohesive phases corresponded to "slowness" and wisdom in heads of segments. Young, old, and dead members all played these roles.

The elder's authority was sustained by certain sanctions, of which by far the most important were the ritual sanctions that were part of the cult of the dead. He had no physical force at his disposal. Above the level of the elder there was no superior authority except for the sporadic and occasional exercise of their powers by rainmakers and "men whose names are known." Groups fought, or had recourse to chiefs' courts, but both fighting and taking to court were opposed to the norms of kinship and close neighborhood. The only other sanctions, except for those of public opinion and the process of witchcraft, were those considered by Lugbara as operated by the dead. The dead were supposed to bring sickness to their living kin as a response to an infringement of proper kinship behavior. They did so either at the invocation of living kin or on their own responsibility. Oracles were consulted to discover the agents concerned and the reasons for their sending sickness. The sickness was lifted by the promise of sacrifice, which was performed after the recovery of the sick person. Part of the rite of sacrifice was the communion of living and dead kin, and by it proper relations were restored. This was the process as Lugbara conceived it. The social reality was somewhat different. Much anthropological theory has tried to show that ritual is cohesive, that its performance maintains and strengthens a sense of interdependence and solidarity among people who perform the rites together as members of a congregation. This was true of Lugbara ritual, but it was only half the story. It provided a set of sanctions for the unity of the family cluster and its component segments. Communion at sacrifices made for lineage cohesion. But at the same time competition between segments and lineages was played out in ritual terms. Living men competed among themselves for headship and authority, which were seen by the Lugbara largely in terms of the ability to invoke the dead against others. In a state society, men may compete to gain the approval of a king or chiefs. Lugbara, without kings or traditional chiefs, saw men's responsibilities for their actions toward kin and neighbors as being to the dead rather than toward other living persons. Chiefs existed (and with far greater powers than those held by anyone in the traditional system) but their authority was irrelevant as regards behavior of almost any kind between close kin.[1]

## GHOST INVOCATION AND VENGEANCE

The main aspect of the relationship between the dead and their living kin was that the dead sent sickness to those living kin whom they considered to have harmed the well-being of the lineage. It was mainly the ghosts of the recently dead who were thought to do this: they were aware of the tensions and dissensions within the lineage, and knew the personalities of the living. It was said that just as a father disciplines his son and expects respect from him, a man expects his dead father and father's brothers to take an interest in him, whereas more distant ghosts are not so concerned. It was said that the recently dead ghosts report the ill deeds of the living to the more distant ghosts, who deliberate on the matter and then decide whether or not to send sickness to punish the living evildoer; they then give instructions to the recently dead who send the actual sickness.

The relationship between dead and living members of the lineage was expressed most fully in the ritual of sacrifice. In many societies sacrifice is made to ancestors or gods periodically: at birth, harvests, or other recurrent occasions. Lugbara did not sacrifice on such occasions, but did so only as part of a process of events that started with a person being sick. They believed that sickness was sent by the dead to "show" the living that they were displeased by their sinful behavior. The ritual guardian of the sick person (his father, or eldest brother, or if a wife, her husband) would consult oracles to discover the identity of the ghost concerned and the nature of the sacrifice that would later be made to him. The sacrificial object for ghosts was an animal (for certain spirits and nonghostly ancestors it would be grain or beer only). It was promised as sacrifice if the sick person recovered. After his recovery, the animal was sacrificed at the shrines, the meat was shared among the members of the lineage who gathered together as a congregation, the patient was anointed and blessed and the matter was regarded as closed. If he did not recover, it was thought that the oracles had been mistaken in their verdict, and they were either consulted again or it was thought that Spirit was involved and no offering was made. To sacrifice to Spirit would be presumptuous and pointless.

From the observer's viewpoint this process began with a person being sick, in particular with the sickness known as *oyizu* ("growing thin"), a nonspecific sickness or general malaise. But Lugbara saw it differently. For them the process began with the commission of sin, which was followed by either ghost invocation or ghostly vengeance. These phrases are my translations of the Lugbara expressions *ole ro* and *ori ka*. Literally *ole ro* means "to bring sickness (because of) indignation:" *ro* means

---

[1]This is the theme of my book *Lugbara Religion* (Middleton 1960a). In the remainder of this chapter I go over some of the ground covered in that book; I shall not refer to those passages in it that deal at greater length with points raised here.

to invoke the dead to bring sickness; *ole* means indignation, envy, or annoyance at sinful behavior. The invocation of the ghosts was done by a living person, typically an elder; but anyone whose father was dead might do so. He sat near his shrines in his compound and thought about the sinner's behavior. His thoughts were known by the ghosts and they then sent sickness to the offender. It was said "he thinks these words in his heart"; he did not threaten or curse the offender. For a senior man to do this was part of his expected role. It was part of his "work," to "cleanse the lineage home." Indeed, an elder who did not do so when justified would have been lacking in sense of duty toward his lineage. A man might invoke the dead to send sickness against any member of his family cluster and his minimal lineage, whether living in the family cluster's compounds or not. Within the family cluster were included lineage members, their wives, and attached kin such as sisters' sons. A man was thought not to invoke against sisters' sons living elsewhere: to discipline them was the duty of their own elders where they lived. Lugbara often stressed that elders were "like brothers," and might discuss the sins of their dependents among themselves. An offender would then be controlled by his own elder, even if another elder was the person who had been insulted or injured. The principle was that a senior man had the duty to maintain his authority over all members of his family cluster, whether or not they were members of his agnatic lineage. He had also authority, particularly in lineage matters though perhaps not in petty family matters, over all members of his lineage who lived elsewhere. In theory, invocation might be by any man whose father was dead, even if he was a minor, and I knew of cases of invocation by a child. But typically it was by a senior man, either an elder or the head of a family segment within the family cluster. Invocation might also be by a woman whose mother was dead; but this was rare.

A living man was thought to invoke the dead because he felt the sentiment of indignation over sin. The dead were also believed to be able to send sickness without invocation, on their own account. This was ghostly vengeance, *ori ka*. It was thought that the dead might think their dependents did not sacrifice to them often enough or did not remember them with respect, and they then sent sickness to them.

## ORACLES

For the Lugbara, this whole process started with the commission of a sin, followed by ghost invocation or ghostly vengeance, followed by sickness. Since ghost invocation and ghostly vengeance were mystical processes, it was necessary to have a means of discovering which of the ghosts were sending sickness, the reasons for their doing so, and the nature of the sacrifice they wanted made to them. For the outside observer, the process began with sickness coming to a person, who had then to decide the reasons for it. In order to discover the "facts" behind the sickness, oracles were consulted, either by the sick person or, more usually, on his behalf by his ritual guardian. The ritual guardian was either his elder or the head of his family, and thus might in fact be the same person who had invoked the dead against him.

Oracles *(andri)* were said to have been given to men by Spirit so that they could discover the "words" of the dead. They could tell whether sickness were sent to a person by the dead, by Spirit, by witches or sorcerers, or by spirits. Oracles knew the identity of the dead responsible, but not of witches or sorcerers—to discover their identity a man had to consult a diviner. There were several kinds of oracles, most of which were found throughout Lugbaraland. The most common, and the first always consulted, was the *acife,* or rubbing-stick oracle. The rubbing stick consisted merely of a stalk of sorghum held in the operator's left hand and rubbed by a twist of grass or even by the fingers of the other hand. As it was rubbed the names of suspected agents of the sickness were put to it by the operator. When his fingers would stick by their pressure the oracle was thought to have given that particular name. There were variants of the actual operation but they were all similar. Any man whose father were dead might operate his own rubbing-stick oracle, although a man would not do so for his own sickness; it was usual for an operator of another lineage to be consulted. It might seem that an operator could control the verdict of his oracle merely by the pressure of his fingers, and indeed this could be done. But it would hardly be necessary because it was irrelevant. The important point was that an oracle agreed with or denied only those names put before it. The names were chosen by the client, and the oracle selected one of them. The client did not put false names to the oracle, but only those of persons whom he thought might have been offended by his behavior. Thus by definition the names were those of possible suspects and the oracle would necessarily select a person with a motive for invoking the dead. In addition to the names of people who might have been offended by sinful behavior, it was usual to put forward "witchcraft" as a suspect, without mentioning the identity of a possible witch. If the oracle selected witchcraft, the

*A Lugbara oracle operator. His age was about forty-five when the photograph was taken, and he was a highly respected and honest "doctor."*

client went to a diviner to find the witch's identity. Thus an oracle could not give a name that would be absurd because the sick person's own conscience selected the names to be put to it. In addition, the client gave background information about the people named to the operator, and there is no doubt that a good operator soon realized who was the most likely suspect in his client's mind and might select that particular name.

Other oracles were more mechanical and were used to confirm the verdict of the rubbing-stick oracle. The chicken oracle was constructed of a round depression in the ground, on the edges of which marks were placed to represent names of suspects. The head of a chick was cut off, the body fluttering and finally coming to rest against one of the marks. If three chickens came to rest against the same mark, the oracle confirmed that particular name. The boiling-medicine oracle was constructed of a small fire in which were placed clay cups named for suspects. "Medicine" prepared by the operator was poured by him into the cups in turn, and that which boiled over quickly confirmed the name. The rat oracle was constructed merely of a rat trap of stones. A name was put to it in the evening. If a male rat were caught, the name was confirmed; if a female or no rat were caught, the name was denied. There was also a pod oracle, in which seeds of a poisonous tree were heated

*The boiling-medicine oracle. The oracle operator pours a "medicine" into the clay cups, each representing a possible witch; the cup that boils over first on the fire beneath identifies the believed witch.*

and jumped about on a piece of metal; the way they moved and came to rest determined the verdict. There was formerly also a poison oracle in western Lugbara, taken from the Logo, who used the Azande *benge* oracle, but this had become obsolete (Evans-Pritchard 1937).

The ritual guardian of the sick person thus found out whether the agent sending the sickness were ghost, ancestor, or witch, whether the process had started with ghost invocation or ghostly vengeance, the reason for the sickness and the nature of the sin committed, and the kind of animal required for the sacrifice. In the case of sickness from the ghosts, he confirmed the verdict of the rubbing-stick oracle. Typically, perhaps, the person who consulted the oracles was himself the elder of the sick person and had invoked the ghosts against him, but Lugbara saw nothing odd in this situation, because they believed in the efficacy of the oracles and the honesty of the elder concerned.

## THE RITE OF SACRIFICE

The ritual of sacrifice consisted of various elements: the consecration of the animal to be sacrificed; the ritual addresses; the killing and the offering of the animal; the blessing and anointing of the sick person; and the distribution of meat, blood, and beer among the living members of the lineage.

The animal was consecrated for a particular sacrifice. The ritual guardian took the beast to the sick person's compound, after having kept certain taboos to be ritually pure. He placed his left hand on the animal's back and said that if the patient would recover he would sacrifice the beast. It was led round the compound in a counterclockwise direction, four times if the patient were a man and three times if a woman. The beast was then stood at the compound entrance. If it urinated it was a sign that the patient would recover and the sacrifice would be made, but if it did not, or if the sky turned dark or it rained, it was a sign that Spirit "refused," and that sacrifice to the ghosts would be unnecessary; the oracles had lied or been mistaken, and Spirit had decided that the patient should not recover. Nothing could then be done except to wait for his death.

Sacrifice was made after the patient had recovered from the sickness. It was made at his compound, and he had to be present. The ritual guardian supervised the ritual, although he might not perform every action himself. The members of the congregation, who were members of the minor or sometimes major lineage, assembled, after having kept certain taboos to acquire moral purity. At first they sat around the compound, members of each lineage sitting together as a group; they were given beer by the wives of the homestead, and chatted and laughed together and discussed the matter at hand—whether the sacrificial animal were fat enough to provide them with good meat was usually the main item of conversation. It was only after the telling of the first ritual address that the nature of the meeting became more serious and reverent.

There were two formal ritual addresses. The first was said by the elder, who talked to both living and dead members of the lineage assembled there. He stated merely that they had come to sacrifice on account of the recovery of the patient who had been "shown" his sins by the sickness. The address united living and dead into a single congregation.

The sacrificial animal was then killed by having its throat cut by sisters' sons (who were not members of the lineage concerned). The blood was collected in a pot, the carcass scorched, skinned, and cut up, and the contents of the stomach and intestines squeezed out into another pot. The elder took some of the blood and chyle, some small pieces of meat, and some porridge and placed them in the ghost shrines. He also poured blood on the shrines. This was the central act of the rite: the ghosts were given food to eat and were thereby brought into communion with their living kin.

The second ritual address was then made, which was far more important than the first. The elder took sacred leaves in his hand, leaves that were thought to represent fertility and that were liked by the dead because of their sweet smell and soft texture, and related the details of the sin that had precipitated the sickness. Lugbara stressed that when speaking a ritual address a man had to speak the truth; if he lied, the effect of the rite was destroyed and it had to be done again. The second address was usually long and involved, bringing in much esoteric lore of the lineage. It was often almost unintelligible without some knowledge of the history of the lineage and the personalities of its members. It included much genealogical tradition, and its being made in a heightened ritual atmosphere made genealogy and history into a single coherent body of lineage tradition and experience. The address was made by the elder who was supervising the sacrifice. In his hand he held sacred leaves that he spat on as he talked. He was usually followed by the elders of other lineages who were attending the rite, and also by senior men who might not be elders but were important heads of families. Often they disagreed about details of the lineage history or the particular sin that had set off the sickness. But the main purpose of the address was to bring any lingering disputes and tensions into the open: because all had to speak the truth as they saw it this often led to further arguments, but in the end equanimity would be restored and all agreed on the main points at issue.

The second ritual address was followed by the rites of purification of the patient and his compound. Lugbara said that ghost invocation and consequent sacrifice to the ghosts were to "cleanse the territory" and to "cleanse the body," that is, to purify both lineage home and individual sinner. The sinner had been in both a state of sickness and a state of sin; the former was removed before the sacrifice was made, and the latter was removed by his blessing and anointment after the second ritual address had been made. There were also many rites of purification that were performed without sacrifice.

The anointment and blessing of the sinner were done by the elders and important men of the lineage blowing into his ear, to "cool the sickness," and then by the spittle on the sacred leaves used in the ritual addresses being applied to his forehead, sternum, and insteps (the places where the soul was thought to enter and leave the body). The leaves were then placed on the shrines.

The last element in the sacrifice was the sharing of food among the living members of the congregation and the wider lineage. This was done in two parts. There was, first, the distribution of the meat among related lineages, and secondly, the sharing of cooked food by those who attended the rite itself. The raw meat that was distributed consisted of the legs of the beast, with certain other parts of the body. They were divided under the supervision of the elder and given to the leaders of the closely related lineages attending the rite. These men took the meat home, and on the following day they in turn allocated it to their own closely related lineages, including accessory groups. The distribution of raw meat reflected the pattern of lineage ties centered upon the host lineage. Immediately after the distribution of raw meat had been made, the members of the congregation were given cooked meat, porridge, and beer, prepared by the wives of the host lineage. At this point the members of the congregation rearranged their position within the compound. Hitherto they had sat by lineage, but now they changed to sit by generation. They were then served with food and beer. The sharing of food in this way by members of different minimal lineages but of the same generation or level of seniority—old men, "men behind," "big youths," youths—represented the unity of the wider lineage. Whereas the distinctness of each lineage and segment, related to common ancestry, was affirmed by its receiving a portion of raw meat, its unity with other segments was emphasized by the actual eating of cooked food jointly with them. Here the individual identities of segments were forgotten and their unity was stressed.

At the telling of the second ritual address, agreement was reached among the senior men present as to the exact genealogy of the group. At the sharing of sacrificial meat, men sat according to their kin relationships as stated in the genealogy. A genealogy was not necessarily historically true, although it might be so. It changed in time, some ancestors being forgotten and dropped out, and the ties between others being rearranged. It was in fact a means of expressing, and validating, patterns of authority among the living. The most powerful man was given the senior genealogical position. I noticed, even in just two years, changes being made in Lugbara genealogies; these were made at sacrifices. A genealogy was all that Lugbara had as a record of their lineage history and experience, so that part of the importance of sacrifice was that at it and by it history and experience were formulated and brought up to date, publicly stated and agreed upon, and both heard (in the address) and seen (in the seating arrangements) by all members of the lineage.

## WITCHES AND SORCERERS

Before considering the place of sacrifice in the total system of social relations and authority, it is useful to say something about Lugbara beliefs in witches and sorcerers. In Lugbara thought, these were closely connected with the cult of the dead, although there was no cult associated with them as such.

I use the classical distinction made by Evans-Pritchard between witches and sorcerers (Evans-Pritchard 1937, and Middleton and Winter 1963): witchcraft is a mystical power by which some people are thought to be able to harm or kill others whom they dislike, whereas sorcery is the use of material objects to harm or kill them. It might be accepted that witchcraft as such did not exist in actuality. It was the belief about it that was socially important. Sorcery might exist, as it would be possible for people to use objects that they thought may harm others (or poisons that could actually do so), but again it was the belief about it that was important. The beliefs about witches and sorcerers, even if scientifically unfounded, formed a coherent system of thought that fitted in with beliefs in the powers of the dead, Spirit, and other agents that could send sickness and disaster to human beings.

Witches and sorcerers were known generically as *oleu*, but the word was applied properly to witches only. The word came from *ole*, meaning indignation or envy, and used in the term for ghost invocation, *ole ro*. A witch was thus a "man with indignation or envy." *Ole ro* meant literally "to cause sickness because of indignation," and besides referring to invocation also meant "to bewitch." The former activity was regarded as good and proper, the latter as evil. There were thought to be various forms of witches. They were always men. Some—the most common— "walked at night," often in the guise of a rat or other night animal, or as a moving light; others walked about and defecated blood in their victim's compound. In the morning the victim would wake up aching and sick, and might die unless the witch removed his witchcraft. Certain qualities were always ascribed to witches: they were said to be incestuous and cannibalistic, to be grey or even white in skin color, to have red eyes, and even to walk about upside-down. In short, they were given the inverted attributes that, as I have mentioned before, characterized the figures of myth. Clearly these qualities were axiomatic only, in the sense that a particular man thought to be a witch was unlikely to possess them. Such a man had attributes as, for example, being physically ugly or deformed, or being bad-tempered and grumpy. An ugly man might be merely a day-witch or evil-eye man; he was known by his physical appearance and therefore was not greatly feared. The witch who appeared normal but whose personality and temperament were abnormal was the dangerous one. Such a man might live alone, eat alone, and be generally unfriendly and unneighborly; but he might also dissemble and be overhospitable and over-friendly to everyone. Lugbara said cynically that everyone hated someone in his heart, and so any man could be a witch. In short, a witch was a representation of the abnormal, unusual, or contrary, in terms of either physique or behavior.

No one knew how witchcraft actually worked, but people understood a witch's motive, *ole*. It was said that a man felt envy at seeing others eat rich food when he had nothing, at seeing other men dancing and admired by women while he stood alone, or at seeing other men surrounded by kin and children when he had none of his own. But the sentiment of *ole* was more than mere envy. It was resentment at failing to achieve selfish personal ambition. In Lugbara, high status and prestige were traditionally acquired only, or almost only, through position in the lineage and by age, the two usually going together. It is true that a wealthy man could acquire followers, and if he were also wise or had a strong personality he might become a "man whose name is known." But typically he had to wait for genealogical position to become the head of a family and so a "man behind." Only a few could become elders, the heads of lineages, but all men wished to acquire this status. Lugbara realized that within the lineage there was ideally a fairly clearly defined and ordered system of authority, but they also knew that not all men were willing to accept this system and wait for their proper turn to acquire lineage authority for themselves.

They wished to curcumvent the system, to acquire wealth and authority before their time, to refuse the proper authority of their seniors, to use their authority for their own ends instead of those of the lineage. An elder who was insulted and disobeyed by a junior was said to feel *ole* (indignation) because his status in the lineage was thereby dishonored; but an ambitious and selfish man who had to obey a senior also felt *ole,* although in this case it was not indignation as such but rather envy or resentment at not getting his own way. Such a sentiment motivated witches. Lugbara were ambivalent about these matters. It was generally agreed that a senior man, and especially an elder, should be "slow," mindful of his responsibilities to his lineage and his dependents, careful not to regard a personal insult as an offense against his lineage authority. A witch was the opposite of an elder in this respect. People also realized that a witch was powerful, and that all men desired power, yet they knew that to acquire it by means of witchcraft for motives of personal ambition was "evil." Any man could be a witch, provided he were old enough. Witchcraft power was closely akin to legitimate lineage authority. In fact, it was seen as the same power but misapplied and abused. A man who was accused of witchcraft was offended and denied it; yet I knew many old men so accused who clearly were not averse to being credited with this power.

There were two main kinds of sorcerers who used material objects to harm others: *'ba enyanya beri* ("people with sorcery poison"), and *elojua*. The former were both men and women. The men were said to prepare poisons, from snakes and other evil creatures, which they sprinkled in their victims' food or dropped in their compounds or fields. They could thus make their victims sick and even make them die, or harm crops and cattle. They did this because of envy of their victims' possessions. Women sorcerers were co-wives who were jealous of each other, and particularly of each others' children, whom they tried to harm by using medicines prepared from the placentae of their co-wives' babies. *Elojua* were young men who were thought to buy poisons from Zaire and southern Uganda. When they returned home they sprinkled them indiscriminately on the ground, particularly at markets, so that people became sick. Their motive was a general hatred of senior people who refused to admire their new wealth from labor migration and who insisted on their taking their proper junior lineage role. Sorcerers did not misuse lineage power, either because they were men jealous of neighbors (between whom there was no lineage tie and therefore no mystical tie of authority), or were women and young men who possessed no lineage authority in any case.

## CULT, ACCUSATION, AND AMBITION

The process of sacrifice and the beliefs in the dead, Spirit, and witches formed a coherent system of thought. They did not occur in isolation. The behavior associated with them was part of the total behavior of people who saw themselves as members of lineages, as neighbors, as important men, men who had ambitions they found difficult to realize, and so on. Lugbara believed in these various mystical powers and the agents who possessed them, and used these beliefs in their relations with others, in attempts to better their positions in the lineage and neighborhood.

Lugbara, like people anywhere, had ambitions for themselves, both as kinsmen out to help their own kin and as individuals out to help themselves—if necessary at the expense of their own kin. It was the conflict that so often arose between these two ambitions, the one laudable and good, the other selfish, that lay at the basis of the operation of the cult I have described above. The relations between persons, which were expressed and controlled in terms of the cult of the dead and accusations of witchcraft, were relations of authority and power.

Although not all quarrels within the lineage and family cluster were between men (women were rarely directly concerned) who were concerned with the maintenance of lineage authority and the challenge made to it by men with overweening ambition, personal quarrels normally expressed underlying structural tensions. These were typically due to factors such as land shortage and population increase. Those disputes that were important in this sense were those that led to the processes of ghost invocation and ghostly vengeance; purely personal quarrels tended to be resolved by fighting. I noticed, from observation of many cases of sickness and sacrifice, that where the invoker was senior to the sick person the reason given for his invocation was usually disobedience to the authority of the senior man; but when the two parties were equal in generation and status, the reason was usually impiety to the dead (followed often by ghostly vengeance). In the latter situation, however, it was common for the sickness to "strike" a dependent, such as a wife or child, who was regarded as a substitute for the offender.

Lugbara knew that men were ambitious and wanted authority; a man who did not was regarded as weak and worthless. But men were expected to be content with their proper authority, as defined by their lineage status, their age, and general social position. Many men, however, tried to acquire authority that they should not have, to deny it to those who merited it, and to abuse it when they did acquire it. Old men died, and young men grew socially mature, and to say that men wanted authority is merely to state these facts in individual, psychological terms. For a man not to feel ambitious in this sense would have shown him to be immature. Lugbara said that once, "before the Europeans," men had been content with their proper authority to a greater extent than they were when I was there. This view should be seen in its historical context. The creation of paid and powerful chiefs and subchiefs gave to Lugbara an example, which had been lacking in their traditional society, of men who rose to great power suddenly, and apparently without waiting to grow old and senior. Lugbara interpreted this phenomenon in terms they could understand; that is, as the success of inordinately ambitious men who not only acquired undeserved power but also exercised it improperly merely by doing what the government expected of them (collecting taxes, demanding labor, and so on). There were also the younger men who went on labor migration to return with more money than they should have had, by traditional Lugbara standards. Traditionally, a man who appeared too ambitious would soon have been shown his place by force, or even have been killed, whereas in the 1950s he could move away from angry kin and neighbors and be protected by the administration. Indeed, a wealthy trader or seller of cash crops was regarded by the administration as progressive and worthy of support, while traditionally minded Lugbara saw him as merely ambitious and undeserving.

Through the cult of the dead, conflicts over family and lineage authority could be played out without recourse to physical force. It was said by a senior man, "I cannot strike with my hand, the ghosts must strike for me." The axis of conflict over authority within the lineage and the family cluster changed in time, at various stages in the cycle of development of the cluster. In this cycle of development, the following five stages might usually be distinguished, at each of which a different pattern of authority, ghost invocation, and witchcraft accusations could be discerned.

1. The pattern of authority and genealogical relationships corresponded closely, so that there was little argument over the exercise of authority between senior and junior or between the heads of component families.

2. Conflicts appeared within domestic families, mainly as a consequence of the marriages of sons who therefore needed land and livestock. For a time, however, these conflicts were settled by the heads of families who merely allocated land and cattle; it was at this stage that the lines of future conflicts became apparent.

3. In time, the population of the group increased and the fertility of its land might decline. Older men died and younger men matured, married, and had children who ultimately married and needed land in their turn. Conflicts of authority arose both between the lineage elder and the heads of families, and also between these heads of families and their sons. As the authority of the senior men was questioned more and more, they had to use the authority of the dead (by invocation) to enforce their own authority. Some junior men might move away at this stage, to attach themselves to other family clusters.

4. The conflicts increased in both seriousness and frequency, and were expressed ritually in two main ways. One was that the elder and other senior men no longer merely invoked the ghosts against their own dependents to maintain their own authority, but competed against one another. They did this by attempting to invoke the dead against each other's dependents. The elder was the principal intermediary between the living and the dead, but to a lesser extent this was so also for any man whose father was dead and thus a ghost. Hence, if a man could show that the dead had listened to his invocation against a dependent of one of his rivals in the lineage, this was tantamount to their showing that they had confidence in him alone, and no confidence in his rival. The actions of the dead were known to men, of course, only through oracles, so that rival senior men tried themselves to consult the oracles and obtain oracular verdicts favorable to themselves. This may sound as though they deliberately cheated, but I do not think this was so. The matter was more subtle than that, for the simple reason that these men themselves believed in the truth of oracles. It is here that we may see the importance of the oracle operators, who were expected to sum up the general situation of conflict within the family cluster and return oracular verdicts that would express correctly the general opinion of the members of the family cluster. Only a sensitive and honest operator could do this, and in my experience the best-known operators were such men; the man who consulted one of these operators and received a verdict favorable to him gained his point.

The other way in which conflicts were expressed was by accusations of witchcraft. These followed two patterns. The first occurred when young men became sick because of ghost invocation by their elders: the young men said that the old men were jealous of them and bewitched them. No one would take this very seriously. Later, however, men of equal status, the heads of families, might accuse one another of being witches. This happened when one such man claimed to invoke the ghosts against the dependents of a rival: the rival refused to accept this version and said instead that the invoker had practiced witchcraft. As I have mentioned earlier, the Lugbara term for both processes is the same *(ole ro)*, yet one was regarded as laudable, the other as evil. It was rare for a man actually to say his rival was a witch, as such; rather he said that the rival was "strong," or "walked at night," or some such phrase that implied witchcraft, and if he found that the members of the family cluster agreed with him, he grew bolder until he might finally have opinion on his side that the rival were indeed a witch. As a witch, he would be unsuitable to be a responsible senior member of the group and should be driven out and his authority disobeyed; and even if he had oracular verdicts on his side it could always be said that he had merely bewitched the oracles to give false verdicts. The position of an elder of whom this was said was difficult, because he found his authority being increasingly disregarded and challenged. His only response was to increase his claims to have invoked the dead against unruly dependents, and if he did this too much he risked even more to be condemned as a witch. There were many variations on this pattern; but in general it may be said that fear of being thought a witch stopped a senior man from being too overbearing and abusing his powers of invocation, and that a group within which there was much conflict being played out in ritual terms might appear to outsiders and members alike to be riddled by witchcraft. Witchcraft was a symptom and expression of dissension and tension.

5. Finally, the group segmented into two or more new lineages. This occured typically only at the death of an elder who had managed to hold the group together while alive. If the elder had held the status for only a few years, or if the group had not increased in number or still had plenty of land, it was unlikely to segment. The succession of a new elder was not marked by any particular rite or ceremony. But sooner or later he made a sacrifice at shrines set for the earliest ghosts of the lineage and that were placed in the bushland away from the homesteads. Only lineage elders could go to these shrines or attend rites at them. They were regarded as "big" and dangerous, and a man was shown to be a true elder because the ghosts accepted his right to sacrifice to them at one of these shrines. Once he did so, he thereby showed that he had truly succeeded to the office.


## THE PROPHETIC CULT OF YAKAN


I have given only an outline of the traditional religious system of the Lugbara. During my stay among them they still practiced the rites I have mentioned, although many young men and women had little time for them. But those older men who were Christians still either practiced these rites without making it too obvious to the missionaries or permitted their kin to practice them on their behalf. They realized that these rites were an integral part of Lugbara culture, and were not willing to see them forgotten. But the younger people who had gone to mission schools either believed that the old religion should be abandoned, or had merely lost interest in a cult that was closely linked to a traditional system of lineage and family authority that had itself been changing radically and that they found irksome. It was probably the general pattern of economic and social change that had weakened the traditional cults, rather than mission evangelism as such—although this is not to deny the sincerity of mission endeavor or the benefits that missions had brought to the Lugbara.

We cannot now reconstruct the details of Lugbara religion as it was a century ago, despite my use of the word "traditional." In this century there have appeared various other cults, as responses to external change, which have been in conflict with the cult of the dead. The most famous was the cult known as Yakan. I have described this cult at length elsewhere (Middleton 1963), but a few words about it are relevant here.

The cult was spread by prophets, who were Kakwa living to the north of Lugbaraland. About 1892 they were visited by some important Lugbara men who wished to be protected against meningitis, rinderpest, and the attacks of Arab slavers and Europeans. They obtained "the water of Yakan" and returned with it to distribute it to their followers. These men were later made chiefs by the Belgian administrator, as I have mentioned earlier. They were reappointed chiefs by the British in 1914. After 1914 the government became more efficient and affected everyday life to a far greater extent than previously. In addition, there were again serious epidemics of meningitis, rinderpest, and later, Spanish influenza. The Lugbara reacted by turning once more to the Kakwa prophets. This time, however, the principal prophet, Rembe, entered Lugbaraland and traveled around the country dispensing his Yakan water. He was deported and executed in the Sudan about 1917. In 1919 the northeastern Lugbara revolted under local Yakan leaders. After defeat by police the cult ceased, and most of the government chiefs were implicated and deported. Since then the cult in its original form had died out, and it existed only as one of several spirit cults.

There are two main points about the Yakan cult that may be mentioned here. One is that the prophet Rembe was thought to come in some way from the Creator Spirit and the water to get its power from Spirit. Rembe was a charismatic leader whose power was thought to be divine and above control or even query by ordinary men. The other point is that Rembe introduced a new principle of organization into Lugbara society. Wherever he went the people to whom he personally gave water were known as "chiefs" (opi) of Yakan. They had a second grade of dispensers and officials, and the mass of adherents formed the third and lowest grade. Both men and women joined the cult, and in some areas membership was compulsory. People who drank the water were promised everlasting life, the return to earth of ancestors and cattle killed by rinderpest, and rifles with which to drive the Europeans away. Rembe himself told them not to harm Europeans, who would merely go away and leave the country in a state of primeval happiness and peace. The adherents lived in camps in the bushland, where men slept with women irrespective of clan affiliation. This form of organization, in which neither clan nor to a lesser extent age or sex were basic principles, was very different to and in important respects the very opposite of the traditional form. The promise to bring the ancestors back to earth would have destroyed the basis both of a cult of the dead and the authority of the living elders who were seen as intermediaries between the living and the dead. At first the rainmakers kept aloof from the movement, but toward the end they became "chiefs" of the cult, thus keeping their high ritual position.

The cult died out after 1919. This was, of course, to some extent due to the physical defeat of its adherents and the deportation of the leaders. But there were deeper reasons that prevented a reappearance of the cult. The mass of its adherents were ordinary men and women who found in it the opportunity to free themselves from the authority of their seniors. It seems that during the dozen or so years of disturbance caused by the imposition of colonial rule and the appearance of epidemics, the senior men had to impose their authority over their dependents more and more strictly. This was resented by the younger men, who also had the example of the suddenly rich and powerful chiefs as people who had been able to acquire much power and wealth without having the proper genealogical status. One way in which younger men could rid themselves of what they considered the irksome authority of their seniors was to join the cult. But when its organization was destroyed, alternatives were already appearing. Rather than try to resurrect the cult, young men found the new chances of moving from one part of the country to another or of going to southern Uganda as labor migrants. In either case they could become free of lineage authority, at least temporarily; if they went south as laborers they could earn money and become to some extent economically independent of their elders.

The cult of Yakan still existed, but in a changed form. Yakan was conceived as a power that came from Spirit and "seized" men and made them tremble and talk incoherently. Older men had shrines to Yakan in their compounds and made offerings to it when the sickness appeared among their own dependents. Yakan was regarded as one of several spirits that could send this kind of sickness to people; it lacked the moral content of sickness sent by the dead. Some of these spirits were associated with lightning, earthquakes, and other natural phenomena, and others were connected with Christianity. Of these latter, the best known was a spirit referred to as *balokole*, which came from the Ganda word *Abalokole*, the name of a breakaway Christian sect that sent evangelists to Lugbara from Buganda in the 1940s. Lugbara said that because these evangelists went into a trance when possessed by God they were suffering from a sickness sent by the Creator Spirit. Both Yakan and *balokole* were representations of the external powers that had affected Lugbara society in recent years of rapid social change: by making them into spirits whose power came from the Creator Spirit, Lugbara believed that they could to some extent control them and therefore also control the external forces that in their view wished to destroy traditional Lugbara society and its culture.

# 8 / Conclusion:
# The Changing Society

I have described the Lugbara as they were during my stay, except for the accounts of feud and warfare, which belong to the more remote past. Their traditional form of social organization was a highly fragmentary one, very small in scale and lacking any obvious political authority above the level of small local groups. They lived at a high density of population, yet they were able effectively to control the continual squabbling and competition between local groups for land, grazing, and water. The great use made of religious sanctions kept large-scale violence at a minimum, as was no doubt necessary for people living so close together: too much fighting would have led to a state of near-anarchy. In addition, except for tracts for new fields there was little worth fighting for, since livestock have never played a very important part in Lugbara economy.

The organization of Lugbara society has undergone various changes, as a consequence of economic factors and the appearance of Europeans and a colonial administration. The first major change of which we have any knowledge occurred at the beginning of the colonial period. The Lugbara responded by having recourse to prophets, and attempted to form a new kind of organization that would do away with the traditional lineage system and replace it with one based on the "grades" of the Yakan cult. As I have said, this was not successful and the cult and its organization died out.

Since then there have been several main developments. One was the appointment of chiefs, described in Chapter 4. Another has been the emigration of young men to the richer parts of southern Uganda, mainly to Bunyoro and Buganda. Men went to work as unskilled laborers and sharecroppers. Most of them returned after a year or so with a few pounds in earnings and such items as blankets and bicycles. Most men returned south later for another spell but ultimately returned to their lineage homes and settled down. A few migrants remained in the south and became "lost" to their kin. Very few Lugbara women went south, because their men preferred to leave them at home away from the temptations of the modern world. Many Lugbara enlisted in the King's African Rifles and after it many joined both the army and the police.

The migrants went to work on sugar and sisal plantations owned by Indians, as laborers in Kampala, the capital, and on Ganda farms; they also took up plots on a sharecropping basis in Buganda and Bunyoro. They lived in settlements from which they went out to work daily, both on their own plots and as laborers for local landowners. They had a reputation as tough, hardworking, and unruly people and had little close contact with the people among whom they lived. They grew cotton, the main cash crop of Uganda. These settlements were usually longstanding, and consisted of Lugbara men under the control of a permanent resident who acted as their representative vis-à-vis the local population, and of women from local peoples. Each settlement was associated with a particular subtribe in Lugbaraland, and contact was maintained both between the settlements and between them and the homeland.

It is often said that the effect of labor migration is purely destructive of the traditional way of life, and this was no doubt true of the Lugbara to some extent. On the other hand, it enabled them to maintain a density of population which was often higher than the land could otherwise bear; and it brought in money that in this area, remote from industrial and commercial centers, would otherwise have been difficult to obtain. The temporary absence of young men eased the pressure on the land (as I have said, the higher the density of population the higher the proportion of absentees). Young men might go south to escape the discipline of parents and chiefs, but most of them were told to go by their elders. An elder decided how much money his family would need in the immediate future, mainly for taxation and the purchase of bridewealth animals, and sent enough men to earn it. They were supposed to return most of their earnings to the elder, but of course many tried to keep their money, mainly by remitting it to their mothers' brothers, who would keep it for them. Old men complained that their juniors were selfish and did not help their families; young men grumbled at what they saw as the rapacity of their elders, who might use the money on their own pleasures and on their favorites. There was justification on both sides, and the main consequence was an increasing disregard of the elders' authority and its religious sanctions. The cult of the dead was weakened by economic factors as much as by mission teaching.

A further development was cash-crop growing. Since the introduction of taxation in the early days of colonial rule, Lugbara had to find money for it, and they also needed money for the purchase of modern consumer goods. Their country is too high for growing cotton, and various substitutes were tried, such as simsim, groundnuts, and sunflower oil, but none were successful due to the distance of their country from export markets. However, hides and skins and tobacco were worth exporting, and the sale of these, and labor migration, were the main sources of cash (there was virtually no local employment for wages). Until the late 1940s, cash was obtained mostly through labor migration, but in the 1950s tobacco-growing became increasingly important. There had been small foreign-owned tobacco factories in Lugbaraland for many years. They issued seed and bought the leaf for curing and export. In the 1950s tobacco cooperatives were set up for the drying of local leaf. Tobacco used to be grown in small amounts by every family cluster, the elder taking the money after sale of the leaf and using it for the benefit of the cluster as a whole. The cooperatives had an effect on this pattern, however, inasmuch as they were mostly sited away from the closely settled areas and their members were the younger men. Consequently, young men were able to acquire their own money and usually refused to give it to their elders. Along with the increase in this kind of tobacco-growing had gone a decrease in labor migration. But it seemed possible that in the future Lugbara would earn more of their money at home instead of outside their own country.

Labor migration and cash-crop growing, together with the appearance of chiefs and traders, led to the last development, that of an incipient new class of people who gained their livelihood by earning wages or selling produce instead of by traditional subsistence farming. These were the "New People" (*'ba odiru*). The more important New People were the educated and semieducated protégés of the government and the missions, and the wealthier traders. They were men who came into contact with Europeans and other foreigners. They attended the same schools; they lived in brick houses and adopted a Western way of life; their families intermarried and many of them had ties with similar people outside Lugbaraland. These men were Lugbara and therefore had intimate ties with Lugbara society, but as New People their loyalties were to members of their class, as well as to members of their own lineages and families. The leaders of this class provided a new example for the aspiring younger men who could earn money from labor migration or cash-cropping. The traditional ideal of slowly becoming a respected elder by merely growing old and acquiring lineage seniority, a necessarily slow process, was giving way to that of acquiring power and position outside the lineage system. To achieve this a man needed wealth, education, perhaps a job with the government or missions, and a willingness to deny many of the traditional ties with lineage and family. Many—perhaps most—of these men had seen southern Uganda as labor migrants, and the elder among them had been soldiers in the Second World War and saw countries outside East Africa. They considered themselves to be the vanguard of social and political progress. The older people who saw modern developments in a different light—as stages in the progressive and regrettable destruction of Lugbara culture—called them *Mundu* ("European") and bewailed their growing importance. But the older people were dying out, and the New People were clearly the men of the future.

With greater mobility, greater economic and everyday social power held by younger members of society, greater independence of personal action by younger women, the growth of new forms of social stratification, and greater emphasis given to Western education by both mission organizations and administration, went the gradual weakening of the traditional lineage system that provided the basic structure of the entire society. This "weakening" was of course only one aspect of a complex process. The other side was the greater autonomy of nuclear households, in which household heads acquired greater power of decision in matters such as allocation of fields among its women, choice of crops to grow, how many young men to send south as labor migrants, and so on. But on balance, in this particular society, there were disadvantages, however highly "developers" might praise the autonomy of households on the somewhat simplistic grounds that this resembles an idealized "Western" pattern rather than a usually ill-understood "African" one. It increased the amount of interpersonal competition for land and other resources without having the former means of their orderly allocation in the interests of wider groups by senior members of those groups—male elders in a formal sense, senior women in a less formal one. An elementary family became less economically viable than the larger family cluster, since in the latter the wives could make one another loans and gifts of grain to tide them over temporary shortages. They were less willing to do this when living in separate homesteads and transformed the former gift exchanges into cash sales.

The factor of security was important. At the time of my stay, all older men remembered the chaotic time before 1914, with continual raiding by neighboring groups and the depredations by illicit ivory poachers. They welcomed the *pax Britannica* simply because it ensured peaceful movement over long distances, and the long-ranging lineage system enabled travelers to claim kinship protection. In later years, mobility became dangerous and thefts of crops and livestock, almost unknown before, became increasingly commonplace. It is easy for outsiders to pay little regard to matters of personal safety, but for people living a materially poor and uncertain life in a barely policed country, and with increasing acceptance of ruthless competition, they were of everyday importance. A concomitant change took place at the symbolic and ritual level, as is described by Virginia Dean (1986). Sickness became increasingly attributed not to ancestors, ghosts, and witches, but to new and dangerous forms of sorcery and poisoning believed to come from strangers and neighbors devoid or ignorant of lineage and kinship obligations. Since, as I have mentioned, sickness was typically an expression of intra- and inter-lineage dissension, this development was a symptom of increasing social malaise.

The Lugbara whom I described in the original edition of this book were as I found them in the early 1950s. Their world, which in many ways had not changed deeply for generations, was to change drastically a few years later with the coming of Milton Obote—the first independent president of Uganda—of Idi Amin, and then the return of Obote. The Lugbara were in general uneasy at the thought of independence, which for them meant not so much the end of colonial rule, which they had felt relatively lightly, as the probable intensification of Nyoro and Ganda economic and political hegemony over northern Uganda (and even the spread of Arab rule from the Sudan). The southern Ugandan peoples had for years exploited the Lugbara and other northern Ugandans as cheap labor and sharecroppers; they despised them as "millet-eaters," as people whose men were poor and whose women wore little clothing. The Lugbaras' fear was justified after the independence of Uganda in 1962. Their district commissioners and other central government officials became southerners; efforts were made to suppress the teaching of and the printing of school books in their language; they were "allowed" one cabinet minister but little else; their already slight presence in the main part of Uganda faded away as the Nilotic Lango and Acoli (Obote was a Lango) gained greater position in the army, police, and government. Their geographical remoteness and poverty made them of little political importance in the country as a whole, and they were left out of most development planning. This changed with the rise to power of Idi Amin, who came from the district, his mother being Kakwa and his father "Nubi." He seized power in 1971 and held it for eight years, to be followed by two short-lived governments and then the return of Obote in 1980. It was at this time that the Lugbara entered the national scene as more than cheap laborers and sharecroppers. Under Amin, Lugbara soldiers and police (there had long been many but always in subordinate positions) were promoted to ranks of authority as the Nilotes favored by Obote fell into disfavor. After the fall of Amin, Obote took his revenge, his troops murdering Lugbara men, women, and children haphazardly and with great brutality. Many went as refugees to the Sudan, but their flight coincided with famine; as strangers speaking an unusual language they were virtually refused food, shelter, and medical treatment in refugee centers such as Yei and Wau. I do not know how many Lugbara remain today, but their numbers have declined markedly since the early 1980s. Arua Town, the British administrative center, has become a lively place of illicit trade across the Zaire border and of sudden wealth for those willing to work with strangers and entrepreneurs. I have no further information.

# Glossary

**affinal, affine:** People related through marriage, "in-laws."

**agnate:** A patrilineal kinsman, i.e., one related through men only.

**cassava:** Manioc *(Manihot utilissima)*. A short-term perennial root crop. It has a high yield but poor food value.

**clan:** A group of kin with a common founding ancestor or ancestress; descent from the founder is either through men only (patrilineal or agnatic) or women only (matrilineal). Lugbara clans are *patrilineal*.

**eleusine:** Finger millet *(Eleusine coracana)*. A small grain plant that can be stored for a long period and is a valuable source of vegetable protein.

**ensorcell:** To practice sorcery.

**exogamy:** The rule by which members of a group (usually a clan or lineage) must marry outside the group.

**lineage:** A corporate group of kin descended from a common ancestor through men only (patrilineal or agnatic) or women only (matrilineal). It differs from a clan in that the members can trace their exact genealogical relationship, whereas those of a clan cannot do so but merely recognize their common ancestry. A *minimal lineage* is the smallest lineage recognized. All Lugbara lineages are patrilineal.

**polygyny:** A form of marriage in which a man can have more than one wife at the same time.

**simsim:** Sesame *(Sesamum indicum)*. A small grain that yields a valuable cooking oil.

**sorghum:** "Great millet" *(Sorghum vulgare)*. A large grain plant.

**uterine kin:** Kin related through women, such as mothers' brothers and sisters' children.

# Further Reading

The main sources available for further reading on the Lugbara are listed below: first on the Lugbara themselves and then on the wider area in which they live. A more complete listing is given in my *Lugbara Religion,* revised edition, 1987.

Avua, L. 1968. "Drought-making among the Lugbara," *Uganda Journal* 32:29–38.

Barnes, V. L. 1986. "Lugbara illness beliefs and social change," *Africa* 56:334–51.

Barr, L. I. 1965. *A Course in Lugbara.* Nairobi: East Africa Literature Bureau.

Crazzolara, J. P. 1960. *A Study of the Lugbara (Ma'di) Language: Grammar and Vocabulary.* London: Oxford University Press.

Dalfovo, A. T. 1982. "Lugbara personal names and their relation to religion," *Anthropos* 77:113–33.

———. 1983. "Lugbara riddles," *Anthropos* 78:811–30.

Driberg, J. H. 1931. "Yakan," *Journal of the Royal Anthropological Institute* 61:413–20.

King, A. 1970. "The Yakan cult and Lugbara response to colonial rule," *Azania* 5:1–24.

MacConnel, R. E. 1925. "Notes on the *Lugwari* tribe of central Africa," *Journal of the Royal Anthropological Institute* 55:439–67.

Middleton, J. 1954a. "Some social aspects of Lugbara myth," *Africa* 24:189–99.

———. 1954b. (with D. J. Greenland) "Land and population in West Nile District, Uganda," *Geographical Journal* 120:445–57.

———. 1955a. "Myth, history and mourning taboos in Lugbara," *Uganda Journal* 19:194–203.

———. 1955b. "The concept of 'bewitching' in Lugbara," *Africa* 25:252–60.

———. 1958. "The political system of the Lugbara of the Nile-Congo divide," pp. 203–29 in: J. Middleton & D. Tait (eds), *Tribes without Rulers.* London: Routledge and Kegan Paul.

———. 1960a. *Lugbara Religion: Ritual and Authority among an East African People.* London: Oxford University Press.

———. 1960b. "The Lugbara," pp. 326–43 in: A. I. Richards (ed), *East African Chiefs.* London: Faber & Faber.

———. 1961. "The social significance of Lugbara personal names," *Uganda Journal* 25:34–42.

———. 1962. "Trade and markets among the Lugbara of Uganda," pp. 451–78 in: P. Bohannan & G. Dalton (eds), *Markets in Africa.* Evanston: Northwestern University Press.

———. 1963a. "Witchcraft and sorcery in Lugbara," pp. 256–75 in: J. Middleton & E. Winter (eds), *Witchcraft and Sorcery in East Africa*. London: Routledge and Kegan Paul.

———. 1963b. "The Yakan or Allah Water Cult among the Lugbara," *Journal of the Royal Anthropological Institute* 93:80–108.

———. 1966. "The resolution of conflict among the Lugbara of Uganda," pp. 141–54 in: M. Swartz, V. Turner, and A. Tuden (eds), *Political Anthropology*. Chicago: Aldine.

———. 1968a. "Some categories of dual classification among the Lugbara of Uganda," *History of Religions* 777:187–208.

———. 1968b. "Conflict and cultural variation in Lugbaraland," pp. 151–62 in: M. Swartz (ed), *Local-level Politics*. Chicago: Aldine.

———. 1969a. "Spirit possession among the Lugbara," pp. 220–31 in: J. Beattie & J. Middleton (eds), *Spirit Mediumship and Society in Africa*. London: Routledge and Kegan Paul.

———. 1969b. "Oracles and divination among the Lugbara," pp. 261–78 in: M. Douglas & P. Kaberry (eds), *Man in Africa*. London: Tavistock Press.

———. 1970a. "Political incorporation among the Lugbara," pp. 55–70 in: R. Cohen & J. Middleton (eds), *From Tribe to Nation in Africa*. Scranton: Intext.

———. 1970b. *The Study of the Lugbara: Expectation and Paradox in Anthropological Research*. New York: Holt, Rinehart & Winston.

———. 1971a. "Prophets and rainmakers: The agents of social change among the Lugbara," pp. 179–201 in: T. Beidelman (ed), *The Translation of Culture*. London: Tavistock Press.

———. 1971b. "Some effects of colonial rule among the Lugbara of Uganda," pp. 6–48 in: V. Turner (ed), *Profiles of Change*. vol 3, Cambridge: Cambridge University Press.

———. 1973. "The concept of the person among the Lugbara of Uganda," pp. 491–506 in: G. Dieterlen (ed), *La Notion de la Personne en Afrique Noire*. Paris: CNRS.

———. 1977. "Ritual and ambiguity in Lugbara society," pp. 73–90 in: S. Moore & B. Myerhoff (eds), *Secular Ritual*. Assen/Amsterdam: Van Gorcum [Reprinted in W. Arens & I. Karp (eds), *The Creativity of Power*. Washington: Smithsonian Institute Press, 1989].

———. 1978. "The rainmaker among the Lugbara of Uganda," pp. 377–88 in: M. Cartry (ed), *Systèmes de Signes*. Paris: Hermann.

———. 1979. "Rites of sacrifice among the Lugbara," pp. 175–92 in: L. de Heusch (ed), *Systèmes de Pensée an Afrique Noire: Le Sacrifice*, vol. 3. Ivry: EPHE/CNRS.

———. 1982. "Lugbara death," pp. 134–54 in: M. Bloch and J. Parry (eds), *Death and the Regeneration of Life*. Cambridge: Cambridge University Press.

———. 1983. "The dance among the Lugbara of Uganda," pp. 165–82 in: P. Spencer (ed), *Society and the Dance*. Cambridge: Cambridge University Press.

———. 1987a. *Lugbara Religion: Ritual and Authority among an East African People*, revised edition. Washington: Smithsonian Institution Press.

———. 1987b. "The notion of secrecy in Lugbara religious thought," pp. 25–43 in: K. Bolle (ed), *Secrecy in Religions*. Leiden: Brill.

Ramponi, E. 1937. "Religion and divination of the Lugbara tribe of North-Uganda," *Anthropos* 32:571–94, 849–74.

Shiroya, O. 1972. "The Lugbara: Migration and early settlement," *Uganda Journal* 36:23–34.

## BACKGROUND SOURCES

Baxter, P. & A. Butt 1953. *The Azande and Related Peoples*. London: International African Institute.

Crazzolara, J. P. 1950–54. *The Lwoo*, vol. 3. Verona: Museum Cambonianum.

Evans-Pritchard, E. E. 1937. *Witchcraft, Oracles, and Magic among the Azande*. Oxford: Clarendon Press.

———. 1940. *The Nuer*. Oxford: Clarendon Press.

———. 1951. *Kinship and Marriage among the Nuer*. Oxford: Clarendon Press.

Fortes, M. and E. E. Evans-Pritchard (eds). 1940. *African Political Systems*. London: Oxford University Press.

Middleton, J. 1955. "Notes on the political organization of the Madi of Uganda," *African Studies* 14(1):29–36.

Middleton, J. and D. Tait (eds). 1958. *Tribes without Rulers*. London: Routledge and Kegan Paul.

Middleton, J. and E. H. Winter (eds). 1963. *Witchcraft and Sorcery in East Africa*. London: Routledge & Kegan Paul.

Nalder, L. 1937. *A Tribal Survey of Mongalla Province*. London: Oxford University Press.

Richards, A. I. (ed). 1956. *Migrant Labour and Tribal Life*. Cambridge: Heffer.

Southall, A. W. 1956. *Alur Society*. Cambridge: Heffer.

Stigand, C. H. 1923. *Equatoria: The Lado Enclave*. London: Constable.

Tucker, A. N. 1940. *The Eastern Sudanic Languages*. Oxford: Clarendon Press.